Champions of the Rule of Law

John Hostettler

Champions of the Rule of Law

ISBN 978-1-904380-68-9 (Paperback)
ISBN 978-1-908162-02-1 (PDF ebook)
ISBN 978-1-910979-99-0 (EPUB ebook)

Published 2011 by
Waterside Press Ltd.
Sherfield Gables
Sherfield on Loddon
Hook
Hampshire
United Kingdon RG27 0JG

Telephone +44(0)1256 882250
E-mail enquiries@watersidepress.co.uk
Online catalogue WatersidePress.co.uk

Copyright © 2011 This work is the copyright of John Hostettler. All intellectual property and associated rights are hereby asserted and reserved by the author in full compliance with UK, European and international law. No part of this book may be copied, reproduced, stored in any retrieval system or transmitted in any form or by any means, including in hard copy or via the internet, without the prior written permission of the publishers to whom all such rights have been assigned for such purposes worldwide. The Foreword is the copyright of Lord| Steyn and is subject to the same restrictions.

Cataloguing-In-Publication Data
A catalogue record for this book can be obtained on request from the British Library.

Cover design © 2020 Waterside Press.

Main UK distributor Gardners Books, 1 Whittle Drive, Eastbourne, East Sussex, BN23 6QH. Tel: +44 (0)1323 521777; sales@gardners.com; www.gardners.com

e-book *Champions of the Rule of Law* is available as an ebook including via library models.

Champions of the Rule of Law

John Hostettler

Foreword Lord Steyn

WATERSIDE PRESS

Also by John Hostettler

'Every student entering law school should have a copy and read it':
Criminal Law and Justice Weekly

A History of Criminal Justice in England and Wales

An ideal introduction, charting all the main developments of criminal justice, from Anglo-Saxon dooms to the Common Law, struggles for political, legislative and judicial ascendency and the formation of the modern-day Criminal Justice System.

Paperback ISBN 9781904380511 | Ebook ISBN 9781906534790
Jan 2009 | 352 pages

Sir William Garrow
His Life, Times and Fight for Justice
Co-author **Richard Braby**
Foreword **Geoffrey Robertson QC**

The 'Lost Story of William Garrow' formed the basis for the successful BBC1 TV prime-time drama series 'Garrow's Law'. This book tells the real story behind the drama: of Garrow's life, upbringing and fight with the legal establishment to change the face of the English criminal trial. 'A blockbuster of a book': *Phillip Taylor MBE, barrister.*

Paperback ISBN 9781904380696 | Ebook ISBN 9781906534820
Jan 2011 | 352 pages

Visit WatersidePress.co.uk

John Hostettler

CONTENTS

The Author of the Foreword . . . . *x*

Foreword by Lord Steyn . . . . *xi*

Chronology . . . . *xiii*

About the author . . . . *xvii*

1: Introduction *19*
   The Rule of Law and Parliamentary Supremacy *19*
   Bonham's Case. *22*
   A. V. Dicey. *23*
   Constitutional Reform Act 2005 . . . . *24*
   Human Rights. *26*
   Death and Torture. *27*
   Conclusion *27*

2: Sir Edward Coke *29*
   Early Steps to the Rule of Law *29*
   Attorney-General *30*
   Early Life *30*
   Chief Justice of the Court of Common Pleas *31*
   The Common Law *32*
   Coke on Torture *33*
   Coke and Trial by Jury. *35*
   Undermining the Prerogative *36*
   Opposition to the King *38*
   Remonstrance for Liberty *39*
   Personal Liberty. *41*
   The Petition of Right. *42*
   Conclusion *46*

3: Sir Matthew Hale 47
Background 47
"Not Daunted by Threatening" 48
The Hale Commission and Law Reform 48
Humanitarian 50
Rules for a Judge 51
Witchcraft 55
Constructive Treason 57
Trial by Jury 59
"Ruins of Time" 60
Conclusion 62

4: Magna Carta and Habeas Corpus 63
Magna Carta and Sir Edward Coke 63
Due Process of Law 64
Habeas Corpus 68

5: Cesare Beccaria 71
Unsung Genius 71
Inquisitorial Trial 71
Cri de Coeur 73
Watershed 73
Declaration of the Rights of Man and of the Citizen 74
Torture 75
Capital Punishment 76
Attacks on Beccaria 78
"Electrical Effect" 78
Death 79
Current Issues 80

6: Thomas Jefferson 83
Family and Youth 83
Profession of Law 83
Virginia 86
Jefferson and the Rule of Law 87

Trial by Jury... 89
Death.. 89

7: Jeremy Bentham 91
Science of Law 91
Law Reform 92
Opposition to the Death Penalty........................... 93
Torture... 95
Analysis of Punishment.................................... 97
Death.. 98

8: Thomas Erskine...................................... 99
England's foremost advocate 99
Family background 100
Youth.. 101
Freedom of the Press..................................... 102
The Indian Chief... 104
Spellbinding Eloquence................................... 106
John Frost 107
Trial of Tom Paine....................................... 109
Treason Trials 110
Lord Chancellor 113
Sequel 114

9: Sir Samuel Romilly 117
Self-effacing.. 117
Background 118
Death Penalty 119
Severity 120
Judicial Discretion...................................... 122
Parliamentary Crusade 125
Conclusion 129

10: Sir William Garrow................................ 131
"Billingsgate Boy" 131

Champions of the Rule of Law

    Old Bailey Practice and Changing the Law *134*
    Savage Cross-Examination *135*
    Adversary Trial and the Rule of Law. *136*
    Human Rights. *138*
    Assessment *139*

11: Criminal Law Commissioners *141*
    Terror and Legitimacy. *141*
    The Criminal Law Commissioners *142*
    Inspiration. *145*
    Prisoners' Counsel Act. *145*
    Death Penalty *146*
    Parliamentary Response *148*
    Conclusion *149*

12: Terrorism and Civil Liberties *151*
    Tony Blair: The Rule of Law versus Parliamentary Supremacy . . . *151*
    The United States *152*
    Guantánamo Bay. *153*
    Waterboarding. *154*
    Extraordinary Rendition *155*

13: Summing Up *157*
    Coke — "The Oracle of the Laws of England". *157*
    Matthew Hale. *158*
    Cesare Beccaria *158*
    Thomas Jefferson *159*
    Jeremy Bentham *160*
    Thomas Erskine. *161*
    Samuel Romilly. *162*
    William Garrow *163*
    The Criminal Law Commissioners *164*
    Conclusion *165*

14: Afterword *167*
    Breaching the Rule of Law *167*
    London *167*
    Belfast Murder Trial *168*
    Arms Factory Raid *169*
    Flogging in Aden *170*

Select Bibliography *175*
    Primary Sources *175*
    Journals and Newspapers *176*
    Books and Articles *176*

Index *181*

Champions of the Rule of Law

THE AUTHOR OF THE FOREWORD

Lord Steyn PC, QC (Baron Steyn of Swafield) (Johan Steyn) is a former Law Lord whose espousal of the Rule of Law, human rights and threats to democracy rank amongst the most influential of any judge or jurist. Of particular note in this regard are his criticism of a claim to immunity from prosecution made by the former Chilean Head of State Augusto Pinochet, of the nature and deployment of UK anti-terrorism powers, opposition to the USA's Guantánamo Bay and to Apartheid in his native South Africa.

John Hostettler

FOREWORD BY LORD STEYN

It is a privilege to write a Foreword for a book on the important subject of the rule of law.

The rule of law has more than one meaning. In one sense it is a principle of institutional morality. In this sense it contemplates a civil society under equal and just laws. It affords the greatest moulding force of our domestic law. It is has great influence on the development of international law.

But the rule of law is also an overarching principle of legality in a liberal democracy such as ours. In this sense a state must comply with obligations in international as well as domestic law. The international dimension is an aspect which requires a great deal of further academic exposition.

Turning to the rule of law in the domestic legal dimension it is important to emphasise that it is more than a matter of rhetoric. It is unquestionably a constitutional principle which supplies core features of our democracy. It fulfils a vital role both in substantive and procedural law. In *Jackson* (the hunting ban case) Lord Hope rightly observed that "the rule of law enforced by the courts is the controlling principle upon which our constitution is based".[1]

The constitutional principle embedded in the rule of law is wider than Convention rights. This is illustrated by the decision of the House of Lords in *Anufrijeva*.[2] This case concerned the legal effect of a decision that had not been communicated to the person affected. The relevant legislation permitted asylum seekers' right to income support to be terminated once their application for asylum had been refused by a 'determination' of the Home Secretary. The refusal in this case was recorded only in an internal file note in the Home Office and communicated to the Benefits Agency, which promptly denied the appellant future income support, without any knowledge on the part of the claimant that her asylum had been refused. The appellant in this case could not easily invoke the normal requirements of administrative law, nor Convention rights, which were then in force. The House of Lords made it clear, however, that "the Convention is not an exhaustive statement of

---

1. *Jackson v. A-G* (2005) UKHL 56 (2006) 1 AC 262.
2. *Regina v. Secretary of State for the Home Desk and another* (Respondents) ex parte Anu (FC) (Appellants) (2003) UKHL 36.

fundamental rights under out system of law". It was not absolutely clear in this case that rule of law could be engated as the operative principle, as the decision did not take effect retrospectively; and ignorance of the law does not normally excuse its application. Nevertheless, the House of Lords, by a majority, held that the decision violated 'the constitutional principle requiring the Rule of Law to be observed'. The House based its decision both upon legal certainty ('surprise is the enemy of justice') and upon accountability because the individual must be informed of the outcome of her case so 'she can decide what to do' and be in a position to challenge the decision in the courts. The House of Lords rejected the notion that the Home Secretary's determination had in law formally and strictly been made. This was described as 'legalism and conceptualism run riot', reminiscent of the state described by Kafka 'where the rights of the individual are overridden by hole in the corner decisions or knocks on the doors in the early hours'.

Finally, one must always bear in mind that there is no closed category of cases in which the constitutional principle of the rule of law may be applied.

CHRONOLOGY

1215	*15 June*	*Magna Carta* sealed by King John at Runnymede.
1219		Trial by Jury established in England.
1250		Bracton's *Of the Laws and Customs of England* published.
1552	*1 February*	Birth of Edward Coke at Mileham, Norfolk.
1609	*1 November*	Birth of Mathew Hale at Alderley, Gloucestershire.
1610		Bonham's Case decided by Coke.
1621	*11 December*	Coke becomes leader of the parliamentary opposition.
1628	*7 June*	The Petition of Right.
1634	*3 September*	Death of Sir Edward Coke at Stoke Poges, Bucks.
1649	*30 January*	King Charles I executed in Whitehall.
1652	*30 January*	Hale appointed chairman of the Hale Commission.
1676	*25 December*	Death of Sir Matthew Hale at Alderley, Gloucestershire.

1679		Parliament enacts the Habeas Corpus Act.
1738	*5 March*	Birth of Cesare Beccaria in Milan.
1743	*17 April*	Thomas Jefferson born in Albermarle County.
1748	*15 February*	Birth of Jeremy Bentham in Houndsditch, London.
1750	*10 January*	Birth of Thomas Erskine in Edinburgh.
1757	*1 March*	Birth of Samuel Romilly in Soho, London.
1760	*13 April*	William Garrow born at Hadley, Middlesex.
1764	*12 April*	Beccaria's *On Crimes and Punishments* (Dei delitti e delle pene) published in Italy.
1776	*4 July*	United States Declaration of Independence.
1783–1793		Garrow leaves indelible mark on adversary trial at the Old Bailey.
1789	*26 August*	Declaration of the Rights of Man and the Citizen in Paris.
1791	*15 December*	United States Bill of Rights.
1794	*28 October*	The Treason Trials.
1794	*28 November*	Death of Cesare Beccaria in Milan from apoplexy.

1818	*2 November*	Death of Sir Samuel Romily in London.
1823	*17 November*	1st Baron Erskine dies in Scotland.
1826	*4 July*	Death of Thomas Jefferson at Monticello, Virginia.
1832	*6 June*	Death of Jeremy Bentham.
1833		Criminal Law Commissioners appointed.
1840	*24 September*	Death of Sir William Garrow at Ramsgate, Kent.
1885		Dicey's *Introduction to the Study of the Law of the Constitution*.
1957	*August*	Mallon and Talbot Trial in Belfast.
1962	*November*	Prisoners flogged in colonial prison in Aden.
1998		Human Rights Act passed.
2001	*11 September*	Terrorist bombing of the twin towers in New York and the Pentagon.
2001	*26 October*	United States Patriot Act passed into law.
2002	*11 January*	Guantánamo Bay detention camp opened.
2005	*24 March*	Constitutional Reform Act passed at Westminster.

2005   7 July   Terrorist bombings in London.

ABOUT THE AUTHOR

John Hostettler was a practising solicitor in London for 35 years as well as undertaking political and civil liberties cases in Nigeria, Germany and Aden. He sat as a magistrate for a number of years and has also been a chairman of tribunals. He played a leading role in the abolition of flogging in British colonial prisons and served on a Home Office Committee to revise the rules governing electoral law in Britain. He holds several university degrees and three doctorates.

His biographical works include those on the radical social reformer Thomas Wakley and legal icons Sir James Fitzjames Stephen, Sir Edward Carson, Sir Edward Coke, Lord Halsbury and Sir Matthew Hale.

He has since written a succession of acclaimed works for Waterside Press. These include *The Criminal Jury Old and New: Jury Power from Early Times to the Present Day; Fighting for Justice: The History and Origins of Adversary Trial; Hanging in the Balance: A History of the Abolition of Capital Punishment in Britain* (with Brian P. Block and a Foreword by former Prime Minister Lord Callaghan); the all-embracing *A History of Criminal Justice in England and Wales*; and most recently, by way of the reissue of a work previously published by Barry Rose, *Sir Thomas Erskine*.

In 2009, his book *Sir William Garrow: His Life, Times and Fight for Justice,* co-written with Richard Braby (a descendant of William Garrow), rescued from obscurity the story of one of English law's forgotten legal giants, a story mirrored by the prime time BBC TV series "Garrow's Law".

Champions of the Rule of Law

CHAPTER 1

INTRODUCTION

"He who would put security before liberty deserves neither".

Benjamin Franklin[1]

The Rule of Law and Parliamentary Supremacy

Democracy without the rule of law is meaningless. The rule is, indeed, an expression of liberal and democratic principles. It is the life-blood of free societies. Even totalitarian regimes, which regard it as a pernicious doctrine, feel obliged to pay lip service to it and enshrine it in their constitutions. But they never put it into practice for the benefit of their citizens.

Nonetheless, the interpretation of the rule can be imprecise and threats and acts of terrorism are causing the leaders of some democratic countries to weaken fundamental aspects of it, such as the absolute requirement of fair trials and the total rejection of torture. In these circumstances it is sometimes argued that the courts should act as a bulwark to prevent politicians undermining the rule of law. And, in fact, in recent times some judges have expressed serious concern about lawfully enacted statutes. This leads some commentators to question whether there is a conflict, or at least tensions, between the concept of the rule of law and the supremacy of Parliament?

Because of these issues the rule of law is today more widely discussed than at any time in the past. But its meaning is not entirely clear cut and is under dispute. It is of vital importance, therefore, to understand what the rule of law involves and the crucial part it has played in the history and progress of this and other countries of the free world. Equally, at the same time to explore the contribution of those who have been its greatest champions.

---

1. Cited by A.C. Grayling. (2007) *Towards the Light: the Story of the Struggles for Liberty and the Rights that made the Modern West*. London, Bloomsbury, p. 6.

The notion of a rule of law has a long history going back, at least, to Aristotle who believed that a king who ruled by the law was a better sovereign than a king who ruled arbitrarily. He wrote that, "the rule of law, it is argued, is preferable to that of any individual. It is more proper that law should govern than any one of the citizens; upon the same principle, if it is advantageous to place supreme power in some particular persons, they should only be appointed to be the guardians and servants of the laws".[2]

The concept has also been recognized in different forms throughout English legal history and the rudimentary form of the rule espoused by Aristotle has long been replaced by more modern and elaborate versions.

However, there remain varying opinions about what precisely the rule of law is. For instance, Lord Bingham, former Master of the Rolls, Lord Chief Justice and senior Law Lord, so clearly considers the rule of law to be of vital importance that he has written a stimulating book entitled simply, *The Rule of Law*.[3] Yet he has also pointed out that some academics consider that the term is well-nigh meaningless. Others, like Lord Hoffman sitting in the House of Lords, believed that it is an essential ingredient of a democratic society.[4] It can, in truth, be seen as a binding force in society. Nonetheless, as Parliament is sovereign it can manifestly enact laws that would undermine the rule of law and there is clearly some potential for conflict between the supremacy of Parliament and the rule of law.

In some democratic countries, including the United States of America, there is a written Constitution which the judges can interpret and thereby make law. In Britain this is not the case, although judges sometimes make law by their judgments which can become binding precedents. But, unlike the legislatures of the United States, Parliament can reverse what the judges decide, although nowadays the judiciary is fighting back to defend the rule of law against politicians who argue that in the face of terrorism it is no longer entirely binding in all its facets. Lord Bingham has played a part in this as with the decision of the House of Lords that it is unlawful to use control orders to detain terrorist suspects indefinitely without trial. There is

---

2. Aristotle. *Politics*, Oxford, Clarendon Press. iii. p. 16.
3. Tom Bingham. (2010) *The Rule of Law*. London, Allen Lane.
4. *Ibid.* p.6.

also great concern over the alleged participation of the British government in the United States' use of extraordinary rendition.

Judicial independence is part of the fabric of the rule of law. In England this has been clearly accepted in sections 3(1) and 3(5) of the Constitutional Reform Act of 2005. Section 3(1) provides that, "The Lord Chancellor, other Ministers of the Crown and all with responsibility for matters relating to the judiciary or otherwise to the administration of justice must uphold the continued independence of the judiciary". Whilst section 3(5) adds that, "The Lord Chancellor and other Ministers of the Crown must not seek to influence particular judicial decisions through any special access to the judiciary". That is not to say, however, that Parliament cannot reverse judicial rulings.

In recent times, with their use of judicial reviews, the courts have, on occasion, challenged Ministers, particularly over Home Office decisions.[5] And, when, in 2004, the Asylum and Immigration (Treatment of Claimants etc.) Bill contained a clause placing the Home Secretary above the rule of law, by removing judicial scrutiny of his decisions even if they involved either an error of law, a breach of natural justice or a lack of jurisdiction, it was described by the then Lord Chief Justice, Lord Woolf, as "a clause ... fundamentally in conflict with the rule of law and should not be contemplated by Government".[6] The uproar that followed resulted in the disputed clause being withdrawn.

Lord Steyn, and other Law Lords, had already entered the fray, asking where the principle of the supremacy of Parliament comes from. It is strongly arguable, Lord Steyn claimed, that it is a construct of the common law and the judges created it. If that is so, he continued, the Appellate Committee of the House of Lords or a new Supreme Court may have to consider whether judicial review is a constitutional fundamental which even a sovereign Parliament cannot abolish.[7] His Lordship failed, however, to cite any evidence to show how or when the judges created the principle of the supremacy of Parliament and the argument is clearly not sustainable. He did add, more

---

5. See John Hostettler. (June 2004) "The Rule of Law v. Parliamentary Supremacy", *The Legal Executive Journal*. pp. 24-25.
6. Squire Centenary Lecture, Cambridge University, (3 March 2004).
7. *R (Jackson) v. Attorney-General*, (2005) UKHL 56, (2006) 1AC.

acceptably, that unless there was the clearest provision to the contrary, Parliament must not presume to legislate contrary to the rule of law.[8]

However, in contrast, were the words of the then Prime Minister, Tony Blair, who ignored the warning of Benjamin Franklin set out above. Blair said that, although the anti-terrorism legislation passed in the United Kingdom in 2002 after the events of September 11 in the United States had been declared partially invalid by the courts, the mood was now different following the 7 July 2005 bombings in London. "Let no one be in any doubt" he said, "the rules of the game are changing". He continued, "Should legal obstacles arise we will legislate further including, if necessary, amending the Human Rights Act in respect of the European Convention of Human Rights".[9]

In the White Paper introducing the Human Rights Bill in 1977,[10] it was said that:

> The Government has reached the conclusion that courts should not have the power to set aside primary legislation, past or future, on the ground of incompatibility with the [European] Convention. This conclusion arises from the importance which the Government attaches to Parliamentary sovereignty. In this context, Parliamentary sovereignty means that Parliament is competent to make any law on any matter of its choosing and no court may question the validity of any Act that it passes.

Parliament subsequently did so act thus actually setting the legislature and the judiciary in conflict.

Bonham's Case

In the seventeenth century, Sir Edward Coke endeavoured, in *Bonham's Case* in 1610[11] to give the common law judges power to control Parliament and to declare certain statutes void. He declared that, "it appears in our books that, in many cases, the common law will control Acts of Parliament, and sometimes adjudge them to be utterly void; for when an Act of Parliament

---

8. *R. v. Secretary of State, ex parte Pierson* (1998) AC 539.
9. Speech on 5 August 2005.
10. White Paper, *Rights Brought Home*, (1 October 1997) Cm. 3782, paragraph 2.13.
11. 8 Co. Rep. 114.

is against common right and reason, or repugnant, or impossible to be performed, the common law will control it and adjudge such Act to be void".[12] No judge in the United Kingdom today would listen to such an argument which has never taken root in the United Kingdom and, in any event, Coke changed his views two years later in the case of *Rowles v. Mason*[13]. Shortly afterwards he reinforced this, and accepted Parliament's overriding power, in his fourth *Institute of the Laws of England*. Nonetheless, Coke's *obiter* comments in *Bonham's Case* had a profound effect later on the Constitution of the United States where the Supreme Court can use the concept of *due process of law* to strike down legislation. However, in Britain Parliament's power remains absolute but the rule of law is the foundation of our democracy and, no doubt, outspoken judges, if in accord with public opinion, can have a beneficial influence on government policy.

A. V. Dicey

The basis of the modern version of the rule of law is generally attributed to A. V. Dicey in his celebrated book of 1885, *Introduction to the Study of the Law of the Constitution*.[14] Leaving aside controversy, let us now consider what Dicey wrote. He regarded Parliamentary sovereignty and the rule of law as fundamental principles of the Constitution and considered that the latter has three meanings.

First, it means that a person may be punished, or made to suffer, only for a breach of the law and nothing else.

Second, it means equality before the law and that everyone is subject to the ordinary law of the land administered by the ordinary law courts, including officials.

Third, the general principles of the Constitution (as for example the right to personal liberty, freedom of speech and the right of public meeting) were defined and are enforced by the courts, not by a written Constitution or

---

12. Sir Edward Coke. (1638) *Reports*, vol. 8, p. 118b.
13. 2 Brownlow. (1612) p. 198.
14. A.V. Dicey. (1950 edn) *Introduction to the Study of the Law of the Constitution*. London, Macmillan & Co. Ltd.

administrative tribunals. Thus the Constitution is rooted in and drawn from the ordinary law of the land.[15] This, of course, is not the case in the United States, France and many other countries, but Dicey was dealing with the situation in the United Kingdom.

However, Dicey was not comprehensive and there are some other features of the rule of law which have arisen and must also be considered. For example, having a fair trial is not only an absolutely essential element of the rule of law it may be said to encapsulate many of its aspects. And *habeas corpus* should be considered as another component of the rule of law as should the right to be represented in court by counsel. The right to be defended by counsel was denied to prisoners for centuries in Britain until defence counsel themselves, and William Garrow in particular as we shall see, dramatically altered the dynamic of criminal trials in the eighteenth century.

And are the presumption of innocence, the right to trial by jury and the right to silence not to be regarded as essential ingredients of the rule of law? It is my contention that they are. Nonetheless, it is perhaps advisable not to postulate a precise definition of the rule since so many factors are involved, some of which change over time and others are disputed. However, the rule of law is a fundamental human right and its meaning should be widely understood and acted upon.

Constitutional Reform Act 2005

Of the three enduring principles set out by Dicey as vital components in the rule of law at least the first two are generally accepted. On the other hand, neither a written constitution nor administrative tribunals, such as Industrial Tribunals, are as anathema in England as they were in Dicey's day. Indeed, tribunals form a common aspect of the legal landscape and there is considerable demand for a written constitution in the form of a new Bill of Rights.

Moreover, the concept of the rule of law is now receiving more formal recognition than heretofore. For instance, as already noticed, it was in *R. v*

---

15. A. V. Dicey. *Introduction to the Study of the Law of the Constitution. Op. cit.* pp. 202-203.

Secretary of State for the Home Department, ex parte, Pierson[16] that Lord Steyn said, "Unless there is the clearest provision to the contrary, Parliament must be presumed not to legislate contrary to the rule of law". Further, he added that the rule of law enforces minimum standards of substantive and procedural fairness. Other judges, including Lord Hoffman, also mentioned above, have made similar statements. In addition, as indicated earlier, in Britain the Constitutional Reform Act 2005 gives statutory force to the concept of the rule of law. Section 1 declares that the Act does not adversely affect the existing constitutional principle of the rule of law and section 17(1) provides that on taking office the Lord Chancellor shall swear to respect the rule of law.

However, it should be remembered that by the provisions of the Act future Lord Chancellors may be politicians and not lawyers, with serious implications for the Constitution particularly bearing in mind the statement of Tony Blair mentioned above. The relationship between judges and government which has existed in the past may have been damaged by the Constitutional Reform Act.

For instance, controversial control orders, established under the Prevention of Terrorism Act 2005, have become an area of conflict between the government's expediency and the judiciary's desire to uphold the rule of law. They permitted indefinite house arrest without trial for up to sixteen hours every day for people suspected of terrorism who might never have been informed of the accusations against them. Suspects could be forced to live hundreds of miles from their family, be banned from using computers or telephones, have their passports confiscated and be forbidden to use public transport. Moreover, they are not told what crimes they are alleged to have committed. The orders allowed punishment without trial and were contrary to the requirement for a fair trial for all. They also breached the rule of law concept that there can be no punishment except by law. At the time of writing were deep divisions within the coalition government on whether to keep control orders or abolish them with the Home Secretary later allowing them to lapse. *Liberty*, the civil liberties pressure group has said control orders were not only a breach of human rights but unfair and unsafe and have no impact on security.

---

16. (1998) AC 539.

Human Rights

There are, of course, international documents approving the doctrine of the rule of law as fundamental to a free society. The most famous is the 1948 Universal Declaration of Human Rights which arose from the horrors of World War II. This described it as essential, if man was not to be compelled to have recourse to rebellion against tyranny and oppression, "that human rights should be protected by the rule of law". And, in Europe both the European Convention on Human Rights of 1950 and the 2008 Consolidated Version of the Treaty on European Union, which established the European Community, extol freedom and the rule of law.

As a consequence of the principle of the rule of law, no person in the United Kingdom can be punished or restrained by the state without being prosecuted for a specific crime and proved guilty beyond reasonable doubt to the satisfaction of an independent jury except in a few specified circumstances. In effect, everything is legal that has not been declared to be contrary to the law. Nonetheless, the rule of law has been described as "an exceedingly elusive notion" giving rise to a "rampant divergence of understandings".[17] And those "specified circumstances" which were once rare have recently included the control orders mentioned above.

The American legal scholar, Lon L. Fuller, in his book *The Morality of Law*,[18] has suggested that eight elements of law go to make up the rule of law, namely,

1. Laws must exist and be obeyed by all, including officials.
2. Laws must be published.
3. Laws must not be retrospective, so that a person cannot be punished for a crime committed before it was prohibited.
4. Laws should be clearly expressed.
5. Laws must not be contradictory.
6. Laws must not command the impossible.

---

17. Brian Z. Tamanaha. (2004) *On the Rule of Law*. Cambridge, Cambridge University Press, p. 9.
18. Lon Luvois Fuller. (1969) *The Morality of Law*. New Haven and London, Yale University Press.

7. Laws must stay constant through time subject to allowing for timely revision when underlying social and political circumstances change.
8. Official action should be consistent with the declared rule.

This is a useful list but clearly omits a number of elements that should be included in the rule of law such as the right to a fair trial including legal representation.

Death and Torture

Not everyone agrees that the rule of law includes freedom from the death penalty and torture. However, the European Convention on Human Rights of 1950, which is incorporated into English law by the Human Rights Act 1998, provides in article 2 that "Everyone's right to life shall be protected by law". And, article 3 provides that "No one shall be subjected to torture or to inhuman or degrading treatment or punishment". In my view these provisions are a striking confirmation of the position of the rule of law on the death penalty and torture and I shall consider how the champions of the rule of law appearing in this book have dealt with these important issues.

Conclusion

In conclusion, although, because it is subject to change, there is no agreement on a definition of the rule of law, its importance and significance have been brilliantly drawn out by the historian E. P. Thompson with the following words:

> The Rule of Law itself, the imposing of effective inhibitions upon power and the defence of the citizen from power's all-intrusive claims, seems to me to be an unqualified human good. To deny or belittle this good is, in this dangerous century when the resources and pretensions of power continue to enlarge, a desperate error of intellectual abstraction. More than this, it is a self-fulfilling error, which encourages us to give up the struggle against bad laws and class-bound procedures, and to disarm ourselves before power. It is to throw away a whole inheritance of struggle

about law, and within the forms of law, whose continuity can never be fractured without bringing men and women into immediate danger.[19]

---

19. E.P. Thompson. (1975) *Whigs and Hunters: The Origin of the Black Act*. London, Allen Lane. p. 266.

CHAPTER 2

SIR EDWARD COKE

Early Steps to the Rule of Law

In a sense Henry Bracton was the first English champion of rule of law. He was a judge of the *coram rege* court (later the King's Bench) from 1245 to 1250 and again from 1253 to 1257. He produced, or edited, the long treatise, *De Legibus Et Consuetudinibus* (Of the Laws and Customs of England) which described the whole of English law at the time of the reign of Henry III. This was a task not fully undertaken again until Blackstone"s *Commentaries* in the eighteenth century. It was the most famous law book of medieval times and Maitland called it, "the crown and flower of English medieval jurisprudence".[1]

Since at the time the King had immense feudal power Bracton effectively placed a check on the Crown's influence over criminal trials with his dictum that although the King was below no man he was below God and the law.[2] Also once trial by ordeal had been abolished in 1215 trial by jury began to replace it and, unlike on the continent of Europe where the *inquisitio* ruled, Bracton guided the judges into accepting that the law should proceed from precedent to precedent. Jury trial became the rule with no inquisition and no torture, both of which were institutionalised in Europe and elsewhere, but forbidden at common law. There was, however, some torture by royal prerogative as will be seen later.

---

1. Pollock & Maitland. (1968 edn) *A History of English Law Before the Time of Edward I*. Cambridge, University of Cambridge Press, vol. i, p. 206.
2. *De Legibus Tractabus Consuetudinibus*. Lib. Iii. F. 118, c. 1250.

Attorney-General

Although he did not start out with any tender feelings towards the rule of law, the first substantial champion of it in England was Edward Coke (generally pronounced Cook).[3] On 10 April 1594 he was appointed Attorney-General and held the post until 1606. And during that time he showed great rancour and brutality in treason trials where the prisoner was not allowed to have counsel to defend him. He prosecuted the Earl of Essex and many Catholics before endeavouring to savage Sir Walter Raleigh with the full violence of his temper and ill-will. The absurd charge against Raleigh, that he committed high treason in endeavouring to persuade his known enemy Spain to invade England, was not given to him and the only real witness who might have helped him was kept out of court. Because of the weakness of the case Coke entered into coarse invective and personal abuse of the prisoner. Since Raleigh's honesty was transparent and his cultural roots ran deep, he was constantly able to deflate Coke. Nonetheless, he was found guilty and was eventually executed after spending years in the Tower of London. For Coke, his career as Attorney-General was disreputable but his subsequent role in the struggle for freedom and the rule of law became exemplary.

Early Life

Coke was born on 1 February 1552 in the Norfolk village of Mileham where his father was lord of the manor, after his family had been settled in Norfolk for many generations. Later he was to inform his friend, the antiquary Sir Henry Spelman, that he came into the world so suddenly that his mother Winifred, the daughter of a Norwich attorney, was still sitting beside the fire at his birth, having had no time to get to her bed. He also showed Spelman the hearthstone on which he claimed to have arrived rather painfully. As his father was a successful lawyer who became a Bencher of Lincoln's Inn it is likely that Edward, who was heir to a substantial fortune, was destined for

---

3. For the flaws in Coke's character as well as his great strengths, see John Hostettler. (1997) *Sir Edward Coke: a force for freedom*. Chichester, Barry Rose Law Publishers Ltd.

the law from an early age. However, little is known about his life before the age of 15 when he went to Trinity College, Cambridge prior to spending a year in legal studies at Clifford's Inn and then joining the Inner Temple on 24 April 1572. At this stage there was little to indicate the transformation in the law that he would create. Or that he would become a skilful lawyer, a great judge, an outstanding jurist, a powerful parliamentary leader as well as an outstanding advocate of liberty and the rule of law.

On 13 August 1582, a few years after he was called to the Bar, he married Bridget, daughter and co-heiress of John Paston. He was a member of the Norfolk family whose Paston Letters are acclaimed for revealing the revival of the fluency and vivacity of English language and literature following a decline after Chaucer.[4] John Paston was a descendant of William Paston who was a judge of the Court of Common Pleas in the reign of Henry VI. As a supplement to Coke's existing wealth, Bridget brought him a fortune of £30,000 and considerable holdings in land. Coke was 30 years old and his bride 17. They were to have seven sons and three daughters before she died on 27 June 1598. The marriage also brought Coke into close connection with several of the wealthiest families in England and his practice began to increase rapidly.

Chief Justice of the Court of Common Pleas

In the year 1606, however, there came a transformation. On 20 June Coke ceased to be the King's chief prosecutor and was appointed Chief Justice of the Common Pleas. This gave him the opportunity to become the ardent supreme defender of the common law, and upholder of the rule of law instead of a pugnacious law officer of the Crown, and he seized it with alacrity. His judge's oath contained ringing words similar to those once used by Alfred the Great, "And ye shall do equal law and execution of Right to all the King's subjects rich and poor, without having regard to any person". Coke took the oath to heart and henceforth never lost an opportunity of declaring against

---

4. *Paston letters and papers of the 15th century.* (2004-5) Edited by Norman Davis. Oxford, Oxford University Press.

the King's royal prerogative and arbitrary rule. It was a remarkable metamorphosis, filled with risk.

The Common Law

Before Coke the common law had sunk into such a melancholy state that it led to the rise in the power not only of the Star Chamber but also of the Court of Chancery with its remedies in equity that it used where the common law offered no relief. The common law, older even than Parliament, might well at the time have been extinguished and replaced by the Roman-canon law that was dominant in Chancery and the ecclesiastical and prerogative courts. Particularly as it was also preferred by the Tudors and early Stuarts who were anxious to enjoy strong and autocratic rule. But Coke stood in the way. He was not only the outstanding champion of the common law against the royal prerogative and arbitrary rule, he also believed it was wellnigh perfect thus reflecting a deep seated national sentiment.

He undertook the radical task of restating and interpreting all the principle doctrines of the common law in his 13 volumes of leading cases from 1572 to 1616 entitled *Reports*[5] and four books of *Institutes of the Laws of England*.[6] In doing so, along with his numerous innovations and adaptations, he gave the stagnating medieval common law the transfusion of the new blood it needed if it was to survive into the modern world. There could be no lull at a period of our history so rich in social and political turmoil – only decay or revitalisation. The turbulent Coke was the agent of renewal in the sphere of law.

His legal texts are the basis of the modern common law and many lawyers across the globe have absorbed their law from his *Reports* and *Institutes*. His lasting fame in England, the United States and, indeed, all common law countries, rests on the immense influence of his legal writings, and his unyielding defence of the rule of law in the face of royal absolutism.

---

5. Sir Edward Coke. (1600-1642) *Reports*.
6. Sir Edward Coke. (1823) *1 Institute – Littleton*. 2 vols. (with notes by Francis Hargrave and Charles Butler and Hale (LCJ) and Nottingham (LCJ). *2-4 Institutes*. (1797) London, E. & R. Brooke.

Coke on Torture

To the modern mind torture is clearly contrary to the rule of law. In Coke's day it was widespread throughout continental Europe and, indeed, it is still practised in many parts of the world today. Under Roman-canon law in medieval Europe criminal trials were held in secret and torture was used to extract confessions. Guilt was presumed and "established" by confessions extracted from the guilty and the innocent alike. In England, in contrast, from an early date the common law refused to recognise torture. Pressing to death with heavy stones was a form of torture but to avoid a trial it was chosen by the victim to preserve his property for his family and was fairly rare. Torture was not institutionalised. As early as 1470, during the Wars of the Roses, Sir John Fortescue, Chief Justice and Lord Chancellor in the reign of Henry VI, said that "all tortures and torments of parties accused are directly against the common laws of England".[7] Nevertheless, he knew that in practice it was sometimes used under royal prerogative since he also wrote, "O Judge, in what school of humanity did you learn this custom of being present and assisting while the accused wretch is upon the rack"?[8] This ambivalence seems to have been a product of the conflict between the common law and Roman-canon law, with the common law standing firmly against torture.

Both the Tudor and early Stuart monarchs supported Roman-canon law but they failed to secure its supremacy over the common law, largely through the efforts of Coke. Yet they were able to use the prerogative to permit torture in the Tower of London. The cover up of this after the beheading of Charles I has been fully exposed from the State-Papers Records by barrister, David Jardine.[9] He revealed the frequent use on prisoners by orders from the Sovereigns and the Privy Council of instruments including not only the rack, but the "Scavenger's Daughter" which cruelly used hoops and manacles to tie the neck and feet together, and a spiked collar known as "the necklace".

---

7. Sir John Fortescue. (1470) *Tractatus de Laudibus.* c. 22.
8. *Ibid.*
9. David Jardine. (1836) *A Reading on the Use of Torture in the Criminal Law of England prior to the Commonwealth.* Given at New Inn Hall, Michaelmas Term. Published as a book in 1837 and in the *Edinburgh Review,* vol. 67. (April-July, 1838).

There were also instructions to place some prisoners in flooded dungeons "among the rats".

And such tortures were not inflicted only on prisoners in state trials for alleged treason. Even within four months of Elizabeth's accession to the throne, at the age of 26, she had written to the Lieutenant of the Tower on 15 March 1559 requiring him to examine two prisoners accused of robbery. If they denied their guilt, she wrote, they were, "to be brought to the rack, and to feel the smart thereof as the examiners by their discretion shall think good for the better *boulting* out the truth of the matter".[10] Guy Fawkes also was mercilessly tortured on the rack for long periods and Coke, as Attorney-General and his prosecutor, was aware of it. He even justified it in his zeal for Elizabeth and was sometimes present when it was carried out. However, he was later to disassociate the common law from torture when, in his *Institutes* he commended the first quotation from Fortescue above.

The issue was finally laid to rest with Felton's Case in 1628. John Felton, a naval lieutenant, assassinated the Duke of Buckingham in his lodgings at Portsmouth. On his arrest he readily admitted sole responsibility for the crime. But Archbishop Laud was convinced there was a conspiracy and, on Felton being taken before the Council for questioning, he was threatened by the Earl of Dorset with torture to get him to reveal who told him to carry out the killing. Felton promptly turned the tables on the Earl by retorting, "If it must be so, I cannot tell whom I might nominate in the extremity of torture, and if what I should say then must go for truth, I cannot tell whether his Lordship or which of his Lordships I might name, for torture might draw unexpected things from me".[11] Not surprisingly, he was asked no more questions and it was decided to put the matter before the common law judges for their advice.

When they met at Serjeant's Inn on 14 November 1628 all the judges declared without dissent that, "he ought not by law be tortured on the rack, for no such punishment is known or allowed by our law". In his new role as a champion of liberty and the rule of law Coke added, "there is no law to warrant tortures in this land, nor can they ever be justified by any

---

10. *Ibid.* p. 23.
11. *Ibid.* p. 11.

prescription, being so lately brought in".[12] The matter was now settled so far as England was concerned.

At this point it is relevant to mention that Coke was an early – if isolated – pioneer in questioning the death penalty on which English penal law was based. He deplored the frequency with which capital punishment was inflicted and the consequence that this very often prevented it from acting as a deterrent. In the *Epilogue* of his third *Institute* he wrote:

> What a lamentable case it is to see so many Christian men and women strangled on that cursed tree of the gallows, insomuch as if in a large field a man might see together all the Christians, that but in one year, throughout England come to that untimely and ignominious death, if there were any spark of grace, or charity in him, it would make his heart bleed for pity and compassion…True it is that we have found by woeful experience, that it is not frequent and often punishment that does prevent like offences…Those offences are often committed that are often punished: for the frequency of the punishment makes it so familiar as it is not feared.

Coke and Trial by Jury

In trials for felony in England prior to 1219 proof of guilt or innocence was in most cases determined by the ordeal. Once an accused was before the court there could be no trial on questions of fact – such a concept was unknown. Although of heathen origin, the ordeal had been adapted to the use of the Church. It was an appeal to the Almighty and was always a religious ceremony. One ordeal was that by hot water when the accused had to reach down into a vessel of boiling water over a fire in a church. The hand and arm were then swathed in cloth or linen for three days after which if the flesh was uninjured God had pronounced the accused not guilty. In the ordeal by hot iron the accused had to carry barehanded a piece of red-hot metal over a distance of nine paces. The same procedure then took place with the hand.

The ordeal of cold water was normally reserved for persons without rank (that is most people) and involved casting the body of the accused,

---

12. Sir Edward Coke. 3 I*nstitutes, Op. cit.* 35.

held by a rope, into a pond near the church, after he or she had been given holy water to drink. Priests were paid five shillings for preparing the pool and twenty shillings for blessing it. If the accused floated he was held to be guilty as it was believed that consecrated water would not receive a wicked body. If he sank he was innocent, which would not help him unless he were hauled out in time.[13]

In 1215 the Church belatedly decided, at the fourth Lateran Council, that trial by ordeal was barbaric and forbade the clergy from participating in it. In Europe it was replaced by the equally barbarian practice of torture to secure confessions. In England, however, the judges began to offer an accused person the opportunity of having twelve laymen, from the groups of citizens who accused persons of crime, to determine guilt or innocence. In this way was trial by jury born.

Part of Coke's firm belief in the common law was his approval of trial by jury. Indeed, in the reign of King James I the survival of lay justice with trial juries and justices of the peace flowed largely from Coke's influence in ensuring that Roman law never replaced the common law in England. In his second *Institute* he said that out of clause 39 and 40 of *Magna Carta*,[14] "as out of a root, many fruitful branches of the law of England had sprung". Indeed, "trial by peers" came to mean trial by jury and, along with justices of the peace, secured the future of the immeasurably important lay participation in the judicial system. Although not without the assistance of Coke himself.

Undermining the Prerogative

When Coke took his place at the head of the Court of Common Pleas in 1606 he ceased to be a Crown lawyer and evolved into an enlightened judge upholding the rule of law which was to become the hallmark of democracy.

---

13. For more on the ordeal and trial by jury generally see John Hostettler. (2004) *The Criminal Jury Old and New: Jury Power from Early Times to the Present Day.* Winchester, Waterside Press.
14. Coke refers to clause 29 which was how the original clause 39 was numbered when the Charter was finally confirmed by Edward I in 1297.

Considering the common law courts to be the legitimate courts of the land, Coke attacked the procedures of both the ecclesiastical High Commission and the Star Chamber. He ruled that the *ex officio* oath by which prisoners incriminated themselves was illegal. He constantly issued writs of Prohibition to prevent these prerogative courts from hearing cases which would result in imprisonment for adultery and other civil offences. Using the writ of *habeas corpus* he also secured the release from prison of persons incarcerated by the ecclesiastical courts or committed for contempt by the Lord Chancellor. In other words, by these actions he was undermining the prerogative and also proclaiming the subordination of the Church and ecclesiastical law to the common law.

When James claimed that the law was founded upon reason and that he had reason as well as the judges Coke answered that:

> Whilst God has endowed your Majesty with excellent science as well as great gifts of nature, you are not learned in the laws of this your realm of England. That legal causes which concern the life or inheritance, or goods or fortunes, of your subjects are not to be decided by natural reason but by the artificial reason and judgment of law, which law is an art which requires long study and experience before a man can attain to the recognizance of it.[15]

That, said the angry King, would place him under the law which it was treason to affirm. He asserted that he had the power to decide any case, "in his royal person". Had not Lord Chancellor Ellesmere said, "The King is the law speaking"? After all, was he not the fountain of justice? And had he not made his position quite clear on 2 November 1608 when he had said that he was the supreme judge and that "inferior judges were his shadows and ministers ... and the King may, if he please, sit and judge in Westminster Hall in any Court there, and call their judgments in question? The King being the author of the Lawe is the interpreter of the Lawe".[16] Coke had to humble himself but was not intimidated and responded with Bracton's famous phrase that "the King is below no man, but he is below God and the

---

15. Sir Edward Coke. 12 *Reports, Op. cit.* p. 63b-65.
16. Sir William Holdsworth. (3rd edn. 1966) *A History of English Law*. London, Methuen & Co and Sweet & Maxwell. vol. v. p. 428. ff5.

law because the law makes him King. The King is bound to obey the law, though if he breaks it his punishment must be left to God".[17]

Before finally giving way, James, in an act of bravado, tried his hand at hearing a case in person but became so confused that he gave up in despair. "I could get on very well hearing one side only", he said, "but when both sides have been heard, by my soul I know not which is right".[18]

Dicey had this to say about the issue:

> The fictions of the courts have in the hands of lawyers such as Coke served the cause both of justice and of freedom, and served it when it could have been defended by no other weapons. For there are social conditions under which legal fictions or subtleties afford the sole means of establishing that rule of equal and settled law which is the true basis of English civilization. Nothing can be more pedantic, nothing more artificial, nothing more unhistorical than the reasoning by which Coke induced or compelled James to forgo the attempt to withdraw cases from the courts for his Majesty's personal determination.
>
> But no achievement of sound argument, or stroke of enlightened statesmanship ever established a rule more essential to the very existence of the Constitution than the principle enforced by the obstinacy and the fallacies of the great Chief Justice.[19]

Opposition to the King

Both as Chief Justice of the Court of Common Pleas, and later of the King's Bench, Coke constantly challenged the alleged supremacy of the King and the royal prerogative over the enactment of laws. Finally, he achieved a constitutional breakthrough with the *Case of Proclamations* in 1611 when it was decided that the King had no power to make laws except in Parliament.[20] "The King", Coke said, "hath no prerogative but that which the law of the

---

17. Bracton. (c. 1250) *De Legibus Tractabus Consuetudinibus*. Lib. iii. f. 118.
18. Lord John Campbell. (1849) *Lives of the Chief Justices of England*. London, John Murray. vol. i. pp. 272-3.
19. A. V. Dicey. (1950 edn) *Introduction to the Study of the Law of the Constitution*. London, Macmillan & Co. Ltd. p. 18.
20. Sir Edward Coke. (1640) 12 *Reports*. p. 74.

land allows him". From ancient times kings had issued Proclamations to impose penalties to *enforce* the law. Now James had begun to issue them as substitutes for statutes not only more frequently, and to have punishments for disobedience to them inflicted in the Star Chamber, but also as a means to *change* the law. Not surprisingly given such attacks on the prerogative, it was not long before Coke was dismissed as Chief Justice of the Common Pleas.

Then, in 1616, the King suspended Coke from the Privy Council and forbade him to go on circuit as a judge. Later in the same year he dismissed him as Chief Justice of the King's Bench although admitting that he was in no way corrupt but a good judge. Four years later, Coke joined the parliamentary opposition. In the Parliament of 1620 his voice appeared in almost every major debate, always in the causes of freedom, liberty and the supremacy of the common law over arbitrary rule.

Remonstrance for Liberty

In fact, before long Coke became leader of the parliamentary opposition to the King. In the Parliament of 1621 he proposed the setting up of a sub-committee for the establishment of freedom of speech for MPs and to firmly demonstrate the liberties and privileges of the House of Commons. In doing so he was breaking new ground. But, King James wanted none of it and the constitutional conflict between the prerogative and Parliament reached new heights. At first the King adjourned Parliament and he then issued a proclamation against, "lavish and licentious talking in matters of state at home or abroad" and forbade the Commons to discuss such questions.

The Commons were not disposed to bend the knee to this ban and on 11 December 1621 they resolved upon a Remonstrance to the King to restate their liberties and privileges, and their right to discuss matters of state under the protection of freedom of speech. The Remonstrance was drafted by Coke and claimed that such rights were the, "ancient and undoubted birthright and inheritance of the subjects of England". After a week's debate it was sent to James at Newmarket where he peremptorily rejected it. Coke told the MPs, "The privileges of this House is (*sic*) the nurse and life of all our laws, the subjects' best inheritance. If my sovereign will not allow me my inheritance, I must fly to *Magna Carta*... the Charter of Liberty because it makes men free. When the King says he cannot allow our liberties of right, this strikes at the root. We serve here for thousands and tens of thousands."[21]

Six days later, on 27 December 1621, he was imprisoned in the Tower of London with Sir Robert Phelips for their defence of the privileges of the House of Commons. Their incarceration lasted for eight months. The locks and doors of both Coke's own house in Holborn and his chambers in the Temple were sealed and his papers seized. Other parliamentary opposition leaders, including the Puritan barrister, William Prynne, and the jurist, John Selden, were arrested and sent to different prisons. As a lighter punishment John Pym was confined to his house and four other Members were sent to Ireland. It is said that on reaching his place of close confinement in the Tower which had once been a kitchen, Coke found written on the door the words, "This room has long wanted a Cook". Despite his confinement, whilst there he was able to do considerable work on his Reports.

Coke had entered Parliament in the reign of Elizabeth who appointed him as Solicitor-General and then Attorney-General. In the latter role he was a furious and unscrupulous prosecutor who, as we have seen, famously disgraced himself in the high profile state trials of Sir Walter Raleigh and Guy Fawkes. As a consequence, James I had made him Chief Justice of the Court of Common Pleas in 1606 and later elevated him (although with fewer powers) to Lord Chief Justice of England in 1613. In these roles he delivered numerous important decisions. However, with his championing of the supremacy of the common law he came into conflict with the King and the Archbishop of Canterbury both of whom relied not only upon the royal prerogative, but also on the Star Chamber, the High Commission and the Court of Chancery, all with their roots in ecclesiastical and Roman-canon law. His attacks on the prerogative courts were directed at the draconian powers of these oppressive tribunals and contributed a great deal to the contemporary struggle for liberty against autocracy.

---

21. Catherine Drinker Bowen. (1957) *The Lion and the Throne: The Life and Times of Sir Edward Coke*. London, Hamish Hamilton. p. 391.

Personal Liberty

By the time of the 1627 Parliament, which was to be Coke's last, martial law had been introduced and the country was in a state of siege. Crown lawyers relied upon precedent to argue the legality of the Crown's measures but the House of Commons responded to Coke's insistence upon the fundamental law expressed in chapters 39 and 40 of the original *Magna Carta*. These read as follows:

> 39. No free man shall be taken or imprisoned or stripped of his rights or possessions or his liberties or free customs, or outlawed or exiled, or deprived of his standing in any other way, nor will we proceed with force against him or send others to do so, except by the lawful judgment of his peers or by the law of the land.
>
> 40. To no one will we sell, to no one will we deny or delay, right or justice.

Bracton, said Coke, had declared that any Act against the Great Charter was void. The fundamental law could not be annulled by statute. Coke then introduced a Bill to provide that, except by the sentence of a court, no person should be detained untried in prison for more than two months if he could find bail, or for more than three months if he could not.

Staying with *Magna Carta* and the rule of law, Coke argued that the Charter meant that the law must be executed in the common-law courts of the land, that judges had to be independent and that neither the King, nor the Church, nor sheriffs could enter houses without warrants, raise taxes without the consent of Parliament or make arrests not authorised by the law. Such dicta, set out in his *Reports*, his *Institutes* and later in Parliament's Petition of Right, which he drafted, had a powerful influence in England and, across the Atlantic ocean on the American Founding Fathers, particularly Thomas Jefferson. These legal texts formed the basis for the modern common law and the precedence of individual liberty over arbitrary government. They were written in the white heat of battle in the defence of the rule of law under pressure from royal absolutism.

This battle had commenced against King James I when Coke was Lord Chief Justice. James had believed he ruled by divine right and was not subject to man-made law. He saw the judges as civil servants whom he could ignore as he wished. Coke, on the other hand, believed they were independent and unfettered except by the common law whose supremacy it was their duty to uphold. Coke followed Bracton when, in the *Case of Proclamations*, he had declared, "The King himself ought not to be subject to man, but subject to God and the law, because the law makes him King". And when he told the King to his face that he was subject to God and the law the king struck him down. But he could not obliterate the concept.

With the country in turmoil, Charles I called for a fresh Parliament in March 1627. The elections produced a House of Commons with a majority of MPs opposed to the King. Among them were Selden and the Puritan lawyer Digges, John Pym, the fiery Cornish knight Sir John Eliot, a young Oliver Cromwell, aged 33, and Coke, now elected by Norfolk and Buckinghamshire – "without solicitation" as he put it – and sitting for the latter in which he lived at Stoke Poges. Personal liberty was to be the preoccupation of this historic Parliament which proved to be the last in which Coke would sit. Martial law had been proclaimed, men were imprisoned by the King for refusing to pay unlawful loans and soldiers were billeted in people's homes in order to intimidate the country. Hence, in objecting to the latter Coke coined the phrase that, "the house of an Englishman is to him as his castle".[22]

As part of his free interpretation of the common law he claimed that when the old law books spoke of the King imprisoning a man, they meant that the King's command was signified through his judges. "The King", he said, "can arrest no man, because there is no remedy against him".

The Petition of Right

Coke, at 77 years of age, now undertook the major role in framing and carrying the Petition of Right in the Parliamentary session of 1628. This would prove to be the first great constitutional document since *Magna Carta* to promote the liberties of the people through the supremacy of law.

It was conceived by Wentworth and Eliot that the Resolutions had been an inadequate means of proceeding and that a Bill should be prepared

---

22. Sir Edward Coke. 5 *Reports, Op. cit.* 91b.

reaffirming the validity of old statutes safeguarding the liberties of the subject. As the foremost lawyer in the Commons, Coke was asked to introduce the Bill and when he did so he said, "we have made no preamble other than the laws, and we desired our pen might be in oil, not in vinegar".[23] Charles said he was willing to observe *Magna Carta* but he rejected the Bill and in a mood of gloom and despair some MPs were prepared to accept the rejection. In a strong speech against their defeatism Coke declared:

> The King's answer is very gracious but what is the law of the realm, that is the question. I put no diffidence in His Majesty; but the King must speak by record, and in particulars; and not in general. Did you ever know the King's message come into a Bill of subsidies?
>
> All succeeding Kings will say, "Ye must trust me as well as ye did my predecessors, and trust my messages", but messages of love never came into a Parliament. Let us put up a Petition of Right; not that I distrust the King, but that I cannot take his trust but in a Parliamentary way.[24]

The Commons now accepted that the Resolutions were not sufficient and immediately agreed with Coke's proposal to eschew legislation and proceed by way of a petition for the maintenance of the laws as formulated by the Parliament then sitting. This represented something different from merely confirming ancient laws, important as that was. A committee chaired by Coke quickly drafted the Petition with its long list of grievances and within a few days Coke managed a conference with the Lords in the Painted Chamber.

The Lords, who felt slighted by the supremacy of the Duke of Buckingham as royal favourite, were prepared to approve the Petition in principle but to make it more acceptable by the King insisted on adding a proviso that sovereign power should remain vested in the Crown. Coke instantly argued that this turned the Petition upside down. "I know", he said, "that prerogative is part of the law, but 'sovereign power' is no parliamentary word. In my opinion it weakens *Magna Carta* and all the statutes; for they are absolute,

---

23. S.R. Gardiner. (1883) *History of England from the Accession of James I to the Outbreak of the Civil War 1603-1642*. London, Longmans, Green. vol. vi. 264.
24. *Parliamentary History*. (1628). 348-9.

without any saving of 'sovereign power'; and should we now add it, we shall weaken the foundation of law and then the building must needs fall".

He added, "Take we heed what we yield unto: *Magna Carta* is such a fellow that he will have no 'Sovereign'... We must not admit of it, and to qualify it is impossible".[25] Indeed, the King did not have it since he could not raise taxes without parliamentary consent, nor could he legislate. Eventually the Lords accepted the Petition as drafted although privately assuring the King of their loyalty to the Oath of Supremacy. Feeling stronger for that assurance the King again sent a message to the Commons forbidding them to meddle with affairs of state. This produced an angry debate in which Coke participated. Many MPs believed Charles was sincere and had the power to override them. To strengthen them in their belief the Attorney-General and other officers of the crown spoke against the Petition but they were refuted by Coke. And Nathaniel Rich went to the heart of the matter saying, "we must speak now or forever hold our peace". This was a supreme moment in the struggle for freedom of speech in England.

Historians have recorded that even the most active Members found themselves unable to speak for tears running down their faces at the thought of the destruction of the liberties of Parliament and the ruin of the kingdom. But Coke, although also in tears, resolutely declared, "We have dealt with that duty with moderation that never was the like after such a violation of the liberties of the subject; let us take this to heart".

The King continued to prevaricate but his urgent need of subsidies to deal with the military and naval disasters besetting him prevented him from dissolving Parliament and, after earlier attending the House of Commons in person to deny the Petition he eventually had to accept defeat. With the Petition read aloud in full with the assent of the King, the Commons passed it with tumultuous applause.

The Petition of Right (1628)[26] after setting out a lengthy list of statutes which had been broken by the Crown and the many grievances the Commons had previously raised without success, proclaims the diverse "rights and liberties" of Englishmen and provides *inter alia*:

---

25. *Ibid.* 357.
26. 3 Charles I. c. 1.

1. that no man should be compelled to make any gift, loan, benevolence, tax or such like charge without common consent by Act of Parliament;
2. that no free man should be imprisoned or detained without cause shown;
3. that soldiers and mariners should not be billeted upon private individuals against their will; and
4. That commissions for proceedings against civilians by martial law should not be issued in the future.[27]

The Petition was treated and printed as a statute[28] and the rule of law had become supreme.

In full it is a lengthy but simple document and was a fitting crown to Coke's career. It was greeted throughout the country with the ringing of church bells and bonfires. However, when the King came later to prorogue Parliament he was furious that the Commons had declared that the taxes Tonnage and Poundage were contrary to the Petition, and he gave a new gloss to the Petition which would have been immediately more binding if it had actually been passed as a statute. Members had so regarded it but the King ignored them. "The profession of both Houses", he said, "in time of hammering this Petition, was in no ways to trench upon my prerogative"; adding, "they had neither intention nor power to hurt it; therefore it must needs be conceived that I have granted no new, but only confirmed the ancient liberties of my subjects".

As a consequence the Petition was little invoked until it was confirmed by the Long Parliament in 1641 when it became a settled constitutional document of the land – one of the three great documents of English liberty and the rule of law.

---

27. S.R. Gardiner. (1906) *Constitutional Documents*. Oxford, Clarendon Press p. 66.
28. Elizabeth Read Foster. (November 1974) "Printing the Petition of Right". *Huntington Library Quarterly*. 38/1. Pp. 81-2. Cited by Tom Bingham. (2010)*The Rule of Law*. London, Allen Lane. p. 19.

Conclusion

The *Petition of Right* marked the summit of Coke's career. A few years afterwards, when he was over eighty years old, he fell whilst out riding and his injuries probably contributed to his death on 3 September 1634. He was buried in the family vault at Titleshall in his native Norfolk where a marble monument was erected in his memory.

His shameful role as Attorney-General, particularly in the state trial of Sir Walter Raleigh, should not obscure his achievements and lasting stature. It is to his eternal credit that he suffered imprisonment and risked his life in defence of freedom and the rule of law and their vital ingredients; the principles of public trial, *habeas corpus,* the right to bail and the rule against self-incrimination. According to Carlyle he was the toughest man England ever knew. And even when he was Attorney-General he made no attempt to advance the prerogative at the expense of the liberties of the people.[29]

In the centuries that followed his death there are many champions of freedom, such as John Lilburne, who, under oppression, conjured up the name of the man they called "the oracle of English law and liberty." And his influence on the Founding Fathers of the American Republic, including Thomas Jefferson and John Adams, and their Constitution was profound. The victory of the rule of law over arbitrary power, which he did so much to secure, with his insistence on the supremacy of the common law, was a lasting triumph for civilization.

---

29. Henry Roscoe, (1833) *Eminent British Lawyers*. London, Longman, Rees, Orme, Brown, Green & Longman with John Taylor, pp. 38-9.

CHAPTER 3

SIR MATTHEW HALE[1]

"If you will not permit me to govern by red gowns
I am resolved to govern by red coats"

Oliver Cromwell to Matthew Hale[2]

Background

Matthew Hale was born in the charming village of Alderley in Gloucestershire on 1 November 1609. When five years of age he was unfortunate enough to lose both his father and his mother. He was then brought up by a strict Puritan guardian and, for his education, placed with a Puritan schoolmaster known as "the scandalous vicar" on account of his religious extremism. The indoctrination the young and impressionable Matthew was subjected to led him to become far too strict a father with miserable consequences for his children and grandchildren who led troubled lives. It also caused the only serious blot on his career as a judge. In the meantime, however, at the age of 17 he began his studies at Magdalen Hall, Oxford and on 8 November, 1629 was admitted to Lincolns Inn.

Hale lived through the momentous seventeenth-century struggles between the Crown and Parliament that produced the English civil war, the execution of Charles I, the rule of Oliver Cromwell and the restoration of the Monarchy. It was a time of dramatic events that changed the political face of Britain and sowed the seeds for the future rise of democracy in its modern interpretation. At this vitally important time, Hale played a significant role as an advocate, a Member of Parliament, a jurist and a judge. Despite

---

1. For an account of Hale's life and works see John Hostettler. (2002) *The Red Gown: The Life and Works of Sir Matthew Hale*. Chichester, Barry Rose Law Publishers.
2. Sollom Emlyn. (1736) Preface to Hale's *The History of the Pleas of the Crown*. London, E. & R. Nutt and R. Gosling, vol. i. p. ii.

not having a powerful voice, he was the pre-eminent lawyer of the day and his life bears witness to a pivotal interaction of history, politics and law. His place in history survives because of his understanding and exposition of the crucial bedrock function of the rule of law in the flexible and changing Constitution of this country.

His contribution to the rule of law consists in: (i) his helping to keep the law alive and improved during Cromwell's reign; (ii) his rules of conduct for a judge; and (iii) his written works.

"Not Daunted by Threatening"

In January 1649, shortly after the execution of Charles I, Hale defended James, Duke of Hamilton and Earl of Cambridge, on his trial for high treason before the Upper Court. This was presided over by John Bradshaw who had been President of the Commission which tried the King. "Upper Court" was the new name for the Court of King's Bench and was widely known at the time as "Cromwell's New Slaughter-house in England".[3] In fact, Hamilton had no lawyer and Hale and three others were assigned by the judges to defend him. Despite this, when Hale defended Hamilton with vigour the Attorney-General for the Commonwealth threatened him with reprisals for appearing against the government. Hale retorted that he was "pleading in defence of the laws which [the government] professed they would maintain and preserve; and that he was doing his duty to his client and was not to be daunted by threatening".

The Hale Commission and Law Reform

During the Commonwealth there was considerable agitation for reform of the law and on three occasions Cromwell urged Parliament to change the law. One such opportunity came with his speech to the second Protectorate Parliament in 1656 when he declared "There are wicked and abominable

---

3. William Cobbett. *State Trials*. 1155.

laws that it will be in our power to alter". Unfortunately, he was frustrated by his own dismissals of the House of Commons before they could comply with his wishes and the House of Lords having been abolished.

Nevertheless, earlier, on 30 January 1652, Hale had been appointed to act as chairman of what became known as the Hale Commission. Although he took the chair on only ten occasions and attended 25 of the Commission's 59 meetings his influence on its work was considerable. It was charged by the House of Commons with, "taking into consideration what inconveniences there are in the law; and how the mischiefs which grow from delays, the chargeableness and irregularities in the proceedings in the law may be prevented, and the speediest way to reform the same, and to present their opinions to such committee as the Parliament shall appoint".[4]

No MPs were allowed to be members of the Commission which naturally could not legislate but was to report to the Parliamentary Law Committee. Nonetheless, it could, and did, produce draft Bills. Eight lawyers and thirteen laymen were appointed to sit on the Commission which generally sat three times a week from 23 January to 23 July 1652. Apart from the lawyers its members included landed gentry, merchants and senior army officers. Prominent, in addition to Hale, were Major-General Desborough, an attorney and Cromwell's brother-in-law, Hugh Peters, a dedicated law reformer and scourge of the lawyers, the influential John Rushworth and Sir Anthony Ashley Cooper, afterwards Lord Shaftesbury.

The lawyers proved to be the most active participants with one of their number always in the chair and they prepared the drafts of the Commission's Bills. But the other members had some knowledge of the law, with six of the laymen having been educated at the Inns of Court and the Commission's Minutes[5] show that the debates were well informed. I have been unable to find any evidence to confirm the belief of Sir William Holdsworth that the lawyers had a difficult time with the laymen. Indeed, although he claims that it is clear that there was bitter opposition he cites only one example where laymen appear to have had difficulty in understanding the meaning

---

4. *Journals of the House of Commons.* (1652) vii. 58.
5. Hardwicke Papers. British Library. *Add. MSS. 35863.*

of the word 'incumbrance' in regard to the registration of land.[6] Faced with a complex land law it may well be that they did!

The minutes were written as the Commission sat and contain many deletions and alterations that were added as its arguments proceeded. Its meetings were often lengthy and there were sub-committees of three or four members who prepared papers on various subjects as well as drafting Bills.[7]

In its short life the Commission produced 16 draft Bills. Some of them were read in the House of Commons in March, April and May of the year 1652 and the remainder were presented to the Parliamentary Law Committee in July of that year.[8] Both the Law Committee and the Rump Parliament proved sympathetic but, despite the demand for law reform in the country, they did not manage to secure the enactment of a single one. Nevertheless, all was not lost since the House of Commons later introduced a number of the reforms suggested by the Bills.

Humanitarian

What is important is that many of the Commission's recommendations were enlightened and foresighted and anticipated a great deal of humanitarian reform and respect for the rule of law by more than a century and a half.

With the criminal law, for example, it desired a reduction in the sweeping incidence of the death penalty, particularly for theft of money or goods valued at a shilling or more. It also proposed that prisoners should be permitted to engage counsel in all cases where the prosecution was represented and that their witnesses should be able to give evidence on oath. At the time in trials of felony – where death was the penalty – prisoners were not allowed counsel, except on points of law, and could not have their witnesses give evidence on oath.

---

6. Sir William Holdsworth. (1924) *A History of English Law*. London, Methuem & Co and Sweet & Maxwell. vol. vi. p. 423.
7. Mary Cotterell. (1968) "Interregnum Law Reform: The Hale Commission of 1652". *English Historical Review*. vol. 83. pp. 689,-724.
8. *Journals of the House of Commons. Op. cit.* pp. 121. 124, 130-1.

Legal aid for the poor was considered and it was proposed that the punishment (or torture) of pressing to death for refusing to plead in court be abolished. In line with Hale's views on judicial ethics (of which more later) and with the rule of law requirement that trials be in open court, the Commission recommended that applications to a judge should be made only in court and, if he were approached privately, he should disclose the fact in court and openly deal with the issue there. It seems likely that this was suggested by Hale.

These, and other proposals of the Commission, were successfully opposed by lawyers and men of property and they lost favour after the restoration of Charles II. However, they were generally accepted in the reforms of law in the nineteenth century and became part of the fabric of the rule of law in its wider sense.

Rules for a Judge

Even though he was no orator and spoke fairly slowly, Hale was a highly successful advocate. Later, he was a widely respected judge after Cromwell elevated him to be a judge of the Court of Common Pleas in the year 1653. This was in order to assist Cromwell to secure legitimacy, and introduce a dignified symbol for his attempt to obtain law reform. For this judgeship Hale took the oath "to be true and faithful to the Commonwealth of England, without a King or House of Lords". He had some doubts about accepting the commission but was persuaded by Cromwell's words cited at the head of this chapter.[9] He justified himself by saying that, "as it was absolutely necessary to have justice and property kept up at all times, it was no sin to take a commission from usurpers".

In any event, it was a significant opportunity for him since after the Long Parliament had abolished the Star Chamber and other prerogative courts the common law courts found themselves with greater powers and prestige than ever before, even though six of the twelve judges had resigned from the Bench on the execution of the King. The seeds of common law pre-eminence sown

---

9. Sollom Emlyn's Preface to Hale's *The History of the Pleas of the Crown. Op. cit.* vol. i. p. 2.

by Sir Edward Coke had finally grown and borne fruit. Indeed, there can be little doubt that the Republic was doomed to fail because in the temper of the times it had to accept the common law and make its claims in legal terms that in the final analysis were based on a monarchical type of rule.[10]

Despite having served under Cromwell, at the time of the Restoration, Hale was widely revered and could not be ignored by the new King who appointed him Lord Chief Baron of the Exchequer on 7 November 1660. It was, however, his misgivings about the Bench in the reign of Charles II that caused Hale to write down the rules he wished to guide himself and other judges. Lord John Campbell believed they should be viewed with admiration and reverence and "inscribed in letters of gold on the walls of Westminster Hall, as a lesson to those entrusted with the administration of justice". These precepts, which Hale believed judges should continually bear in mind are:

1. That in the administration of justice, I am entrusted for God, the King, and country; and therefore,
2. That it be done, 1st, uprightly; 2^{ndly}, deliberately, $3^{rdly,}$ resolutely.
3. That I rest not on my own understanding or strength, but implore and rest upon the direction and strength of God.
4. That in the execution of justice I carefully lay aside my own passions, and not give way to them, however provoked.
5. That I be wholly intent upon the business I am about, remitting all other cares and thoughts as unseasonable, and interruptions.
6. That I suffer not myself to be prepossessed with any judgment at all, till the whole business, and both parties be heard.
7. That I never engage myself in the beginning of any cause, but reserve myself unprejudiced till the whole be heard.
8. That in business capital, though my nature prompt me to pity yet to consider that there is also pity due to the country.
9. That I be not too rigid in matters purely conscientious, where all the harm is diversity of judgment.

---

10. See Alan Cromartie. (1995) *Sir Matthew Hale 1609-1676: Law, religion and natural philosophy*. Cambridge, Cambridge University Press. p. 58 And Stuart E. Prall. (1966) *The Agitation for Law Reform during the Puritan Revolution, 1640-1660*. p. 1.

10. That I be not biased with compassion to the poor, or favour to the rich, in point of justice.
11. That popular or court applause, or distaste, have no influence into any thing I do in point of distribution of justice.
12. Not to be solicitous what men will say or think, so long as I keep myself exactly according to the rules of justice.
13. If with criminals, it be a measuring cast to incline to mercy and acquittal.
14. In crimes that consist merely in words when no harm ensues, moderation is no injustice.
15. In criminals of blood, if the fact be evident, severity is justice.
16. To abhor all private solicitations, of what kind soever and by whomsoever, in matters depending.
17. To charge my servants: 1st, not to interpose in any business whatsoever; 2nd, not to take more than their known fees; 3rd, not to give any undue precedence to causes; 4th, not to recommend counsel.
18. To be short and sparing at meals, that I may be the fitter for business."

Hale always endeavoured to give effect to these precepts and a few examples will give some indication of his determination. In connection with rule 13 it was about the time he wrote them down that, with a sensitivity in advance of his contemporary judges, he also wrote that, "most certainly the safest error is to exceed in mercy rather than in severity ... for it may be that the person I now spare may on that very account become a man of great service to the kingdom". And, "Again: suppose a guilty person escape, yet he is under the wrath of Divine justice, that can take him when he pleaseth, when the over severe punishment of one that seems guilty, but, it may be, is *not*, is oftentimes irreparable".[12]

Instances abound of Hale putting rule 16 into effect. When a Duke approached him in his chambers in order, he said, to help the judge understand a case that was to come before him at Aylesbury, Hale told him that

---

11. See Bishop Gilbert Burnett. (1856) *The Life and Death of Sir Matthew Hale*. Oxford, Oxford University Press. p. 35-6.
12. Sir John Bickerton Williams. (1835) *The Memoirs of the Life, Character and Writings of Sir Matthew Hale*. London, p. 76.

he received information about cases only in open court. When the Duke complained to the King that he had suffered a rudeness not to be endured he was told to content himself that he was not used worse.

On another occasion the Chief Baron was sent a buck by a party to a case. On noticing the name of the litigant when the case commenced, Hale asked if he was the man who had sent the venison. On learning that he was he told him that the trial could not proceed until he had paid him for it. The offender then remarked that, "he never sold his venison, and that he had done nothing to *him* that he did not do to every judge that had gone the circuit".[13] This was known to be true but Hale nevertheless withdrew from the case. He had learned from Solomon, he said, that "a gift perverted the ways of Judgment".

An extraordinary story of about this time was told later in the *Gentleman's Magazine*. Hale was sitting on the trial of a poor young man who was cast upon the shores of Cornwall and in great hunger opened a window and took out a loaf. On his trial the jury found him guilty of burglary which bore the death penalty and it was with great difficulty that Hale persuaded the jurors to change their verdict to an acquittal.

Some years afterwards Hale was being sumptuously entertained on the Northern Circuit and he reproved the sheriff for setting so bad an example. The sheriff replied that he would not have done so much for any other judge but, "for your Lordship I can never do too much. You saved my life". Asked how that was so, he said, I was arraigned before you and you sent out the jury again and again until they acquitted me". "Are you the man", asked Hale, "who was arraigned for stealing the loaf". "The very same man", replied the sheriff, and "since then a great estate is fallen to me, and I am in the post you see". [14]

In giving effect to his own rules for a judge Hale also enhanced important features of the rule of law. Indeed, these precepts were regarded as a milestone in the history of the rule of law by Lord Bingham.[15]

---

13. *Ibid.* p. 102.
14. *Gentleman's Magazine*. vol. 13. (July 1851)
15. Tom Bingham. (2010) *The Rule of Law*. London, Allen Lane, p. 20.

Sir Matthew Hale

Witchcraft

The only example I have found in which Hale did not act on his own precepts was the case of two elderly widows, Rose Callender and Amy Duny who were brought to trial before him as Lord Chief Baron. They were charged with witchcraft at the Bury St Edmunds Assizes in Suffolk on 10 March 1665.[16] Seven children, who were too young, or allegedly too ill, to give evidence themselves were said by the prosecution to have been bewitched by the prisoners. Three of them appeared in the courtroom falling into violent fits and shrieking before their parents claimed that they were struck dumb. This is unlikely but, in any event, they did not speak until after the women were convicted when suddenly they recovered their voices. Some of the alleged bewitching took place six or seven years before the trial and evidence was given by the parents of the children that, for example, when a toad was thrown into the fire in a house it made "a great and horrible noise followed by a flashing in the fire like gunpowder" before it finally disappeared.

It was testified that some of the children vomited up large numbers of pins, that they saw invisible mice and an invisible duck and one child had claimed to have had a nail put in her mouth by a bee, which was really a witch. Serjeant John Kelyng, who was present in court and later became Chief Justice of the King's Bench, said he was "much dissatisfied" with the evidence which was not sufficient to convict the prisoners. He declared that they should not be found guilty upon "the imagination of the parties bewitched. For if that might be allowed, no person whatsoever can be in safety, for perhaps they might fancy another person, who might altogether be innocent in such matters".[17]

Hale arranged for a test to be made by Kelyng and two other prominent persons in court. It was also claimed that some of the children had clenched fists which could be opened only by one of the prisoners. To test the truth of this one of the children was blindfolded and in the presence of the three men she was touched by an independent person and immediately opened her hand. The three gentlemen informed Hale that they believed the whole

---

16. Cobbett's *State Trials*. (1810) London, R. Bagshaw. vol. vi. p. 647.
17. *Ibid.* p. 697.

transaction was a mere imposture. At the end of the prosecution case the prisoners, who were poorly educated and unrepresented, had little to say beyond denying the charges.

Hale then addressed the jury and put his biblical fundamentalism before the rule of law and his own precepts. Contrary also to judicial custom he said he would not sum up the evidence for fear he would misinterpret it on one side or the other. He then told them that there was no doubt there were such creatures as witches. The scriptures affirmed it.[18] Furthermore, the wisdom of all nations had provided laws against such persons which showed their confidence in such a crime.[19] Although Hale took the Bible literally he should not have taken seriously the tissue of lies, children's fantasies and pitiful "proofs" of witchcraft in the case, particularly as not all his brother judges at the time were equally disposed to heed such nonsense and dispense justice from the Bible.

At the end of the trial the prisoners were found guilty and immediately all the children (with one exception) were restored to full health and slept well that night with no pain. The two women were sentenced by Hale to be hanged and were executed on 17 March 1664 still protesting their innocence. Once the jury found the women guilty Hale was bound to pronounce the sentence of death provided by statute. But he could have attempted to influence the jury in this case as he had in other trials in the past. However, as Mr Justice Foster put it "This great and good man was betrayed, notwithstanding the rectitude of his intentions, into a great mistake, under the strong bias of early prejudices".[20] Nevertheless it was a wretched episode that was the single blot on Hale's integrity and distinguished career. His strict Puritan upbringing and his unhealthy religious certitude had betrayed him.

---

18. Chapter 22:18 of the *Book of Exodus* says "Thou shall not suffer a witch to live". And chapter 20:27 of *Leviticus* says "A man also or a woman that hath a familiar spirit, or that is a wizard, shall surely be put to death; they shall stone them with stones; their blood *shall be* upon them".
19. Cobbett's *State Trials*. (1809-1828) London, R. Bagshaw. p. 700.
20. Sir Michael Foster. (1762) *A Report of some Proceedings on the Commission of Oyez and Terminer and Gaol Delivery for the Trial of the Rebels in 1746*. Preface. Oxford, The Clarendon Press. vol. vii.

Sir Matthew Hale

Constructive Treason

Apart from this terrible violation of justice, Hale also made a contribution to the rule of law both as a jurist and a judge. His *History of the Pleas of the Crown*[21] in two volumes, although uncompleted at his death, is a comprehensive historical account of the law and procedure in trials of treason and felony in his day and brings up to date the *Reports* and *Institutes* of Coke.

One instance was the trial of Messenger and Beasley, known as "The Apprentices' Case".[22] This involved the vexed question of whether an assembly was a riot, which was a felony, or a constructive levying of war against the King within his realm, which was high treason. The problem caused Hale much trouble. He accepted that an assembly actually to levy war against the King, either to depose him or restrain or force him to do any act or to remove his counsellors or ministers, was an overt act proving the compassing (imagining) of the death of the King under the Treason Act of 1352. But what, he asked, if there was a levying of war against the King merely by interpretation and construction of the law? The courts had already held that raising a force to destroy a particular enclosure was a riot only whereas to go from town to town to destroy all enclosures was treason on the ground that to attempt to overthrow the King's laws was to levy war against him.[23]

Hale refused to accept that this was the true situation in *Messenger's Case*. Here he stood out against ten of his brother judges, led by Sir John Kelyng, by now Lord Chief Justice of the King's Bench, in holding that the rioting in this case was not treason. Kelyng told the jury that the prisoners were guilty of treason and added, "We must make this for a public example, for we are but newly delivered from rebellion and we know how that rebellion first began under pretence of religion and the law; for the devil hath always this vizor". He defined treason in this way:

> By levying of war is meant not only when a body is gathered together as when an army is, but if a company of people will go about any public reformation, that is

---

21. Sir Matthew Hale. (1736) *The History of the Pleas of the Crown*. London, E. And R. Nutt and R. Gosling.
22. William Cobbet's *State Trials*. (1809-1828) London, R. Bagshaw.. vol. vi. col. 879.
23. *Bradshaw's Case*. (1597) Coke. 3 *Institute*. 9-10, 1644.

High Treason...for they take upon them the royal authority; the way is worse than the thing. These men do pretend that their design was against bawdy houses; now for men to go about to pull down houses with a captain and an ensign and weapons; if this thing be endured, who is safe? It is High Treason because it doth betray the peace of the nation...for if every man may reform what he will, no man is safe.

But Hale would not agree that the riot was even remotely evidence of an overt act to prove levying public war against the King and compassing his death – the true meaning of treason. He saw only an unruly group of London apprentices among whom an Easter Monday custom of pulling down bawdy houses had long existed. Although there were several hundred of them, and a man named Beasley led them with an upraised sword, Hale said he believed they meant to destroy two or three brothels in Moorfields at most and that in any event the statute 1 Mar. c. 12, although discontinued, had made an assembly of more than twelve persons only felony, not treason.

In the event, eight of the fourteen prisoners were found guilty of whom four were executed. The celebrated Mr. Justice Forster argued subsequently that the case had perverted the law and had been fit only for the Star Chamber. The opinion of Hale, he said, was worth that of a host of his brethren, "and if weight and not number will establish truth, his reasoning must prevail".[24]

Hale had to accept that it was constructive treason to attempt to pull down enclosures, to enhance servants' wages or alter the established religion. These cases being settled, he said,

> ...we must acquiesce in them; but in my opinion, if new cases happen for the future, that have not an express resolution in point, nor are expressly within the words of 25 E. 3. [the Treason Act of 1352] though they may seem to have a parity of reason, it is the safest way, and most agreeable to the wisdom of the great Act of 25 E. 3, first to consult the Parliament and have their declaration and to be very wary of multiplying constructive and interpretative treasons, for we know not where it will end.[25]

In fact the Treason Act of 1352 had specifically provided that it should not be extended other than by statute but in time the judges ignored this provision.

---

24. William Cobbett's. *State Trials. Op. cit.* 910.
25. Matthew Hale. *The History of the Pleas of the Crown. Op. cit.* vol. i. p. 132.

Hale seems, however, to have made his point with *Messenger's Case*. Seven years later, when he and other judges were asked to give an opinion on a riot by several hundred weavers in London who had violently broken into homes to destroy engine-looms which they considered were taking away their jobs, the judges were divided five against five and induced the prosecution to proceed for riot only and not for treason on the ground that it was a domestic dispute.

Trial by Jury

Hale also wrote on trial by jury in his book, *A History of the Common Law of England*.[26] It was, he enthused, "the best mode of trial in the world". The twelve jurors were sworn to try the case according to the evidence in open court with witnesses sworn and giving oral evidence. Written evidence was not acceptable because too often

> ... a crafty Clerk, Commissioner or Examiner will make a witness speak what he truly never meant by his dressing of it up in his own Terms, Phrases and Expressions; whereas on the other Hand, many times the very Manner of a witnesses's delivering his Testimony will give a probable Indication whether he speaks truly or falsely.

Here Hale was speaking from personal knowledge as an advocate and judge and was dismissing the prevalence of documentary witness statements in use on the continent of Europe. During the course of the case, he wrote, the judge, members of the jury, the parties and advocates were permitted to ask questions of the witnesses which "beats and boults out the Truth much better". Nevertheless, the judge should ensure that witnesses were treated with patience and not subjected to bullying that could produce nervousness and confusion and defeat the ends of justice. This was, however, a principle more honoured in the breach than in observance by most other judges. He also claimed that the parties were allowed to be represented by lawyers but although this was true of civil cases and trials of misdemeanours it was

---

26. Sir Matthew Hale. (1739) *The History of the Common Law*. London, T. Waller.

not true of trials for high treason and the many cases of felony of which attracted the death penalty.

"Ruins of Time"

Andrew Amos was one of the five Criminal Law Commissioners appointed by Lord Chancellor Brougham in 1833 to codify and reform the English criminal law. Twenty three years later he was to make a serious and learned criticism of Hale's *Pleas of the Crown* in a book published in 1856 and entitled, *Ruins of Time exemplified in Sir Matthew Hale's History of the Pleas of the Crown*.

Amos considered Hale's work to be, "the most famous book ever published on the subject of the English criminal law".[27] It had, he said, no rival for authority, influence and reputation. By way of contrast, he wrote, subsequent attempts to keep pace with the "rapid vegetation" of the criminal law were to be compared with the operations of the slow barber of antiquity whose customers' beards grew again before he had done shaving. That problem could, of course, not be laid at Hale's door. Nevertheless, Amos went on to claim that Hale's eminence had caused a number of later writers to give some decisions of "mean and odious origin" an importance they did not deserve simply because Hale had recorded them as precedents.

They were, he wrote, "like insects in amber, which are themselves neither rich nor rare, but which are made precious by the mausoleum wherein they are entombed". Moreover, Hale had chiefly relied upon the treatises of Staundforde and Michael Dalton as well as the *Third Institute* of Sir Edward Coke. Added to these were statutes and a few interesting cases of Hale's own when he was a judge. In doing so, claimed Amos, Hale had sanctified established doctrines that were an affront to common sense and abhorrent to humanity, without any disapproval or sign that his feelings were shocked. He could, Amos complained, dismiss a man to his home and a woman to

---

27. Andrew Amos. (1856) *The Ruins of Time exemplified in Sir Matthew Hale's Pleas of the Crown*. London, V. & R. Stevens and G. S. Norton. Preface. xxiii. Other extracts from the book are taken from the same edition.

the gallows for similar crimes without comment beyond that the different treatments resulted from the law of clergy.

However, the benefit of clergy had a long history in the annals of criminal law and it was not available to convicted women except for certain relatively minor offences. Furthermore, Hale was not as inclined, or in a position, to press his own interpretation of, or gloss upon, the law as Coke had been. After all, Coke had relied upon a widespread ignorance of the law which, largely as a result of his efforts, no longer existed in Hale's day. Moreover, the times in which Hale lived were not as enlightened in regard to punishments as those of Amos (and they were not particularly enlightened then). And it should be remembered that Hale did express concern about capital punishment and miscarriages of justice and as a judge he frequently endeavoured to help those suffering from legal disabilities.

Disregarding what he had earlier called the "rapid vegetation" of the criminal law, Amos, somewhat inconsistently, concluded that since Hale's time the law had been transformed. This was indeed true. Among other things, benefit of clergy had been abolished; many of the inconsistencies in the common law had been washed away by subsequent decisions of the courts; judges were independent; prisoners could engage counsel; the incidence of capital punishment had been considerably reduced; and juries were no longer packed or punished. If a treatise written in the reign of Charles II did not contain laws and opinions that were obsolete by the reign of Queen Victoria it would have represented a failure in human progress.

In his book Amos could not admit to any virtue in judge-made law or the doctrine of precedent. As a Benthamite he wanted all law to be cut and dried in an original and virtually unalterable code. So remarkable was the code of criminal law that Bentham had proposed that he said it would need amendment only once every hundred years. It remains quite true that Hale might have taken a more liberal stand in relation to the worst aspects of criminal law and punishments. But to say that in setting down, explaining and attempting to improve the law as it was Hale should also have launched a public attack upon it was to ignore reality and the true value of both his writings and his work for law reform. Overall, Hale's conduct as a judge and his rules for judges, his work on the Hale Commission and his recording of the expanding common law all contributed to a growing understanding of the rule of law. That is why, like the works of Coke, Hale's *Pleas of the Crown* had to be hidden away from royal destruction and published only sixty year after his death.

Conclusion

After a period of fragile health, Hale died at Alderley House on Christmas Day, 1676. He was buried in Alderley churchyard where his widow was later buried in 1694 and where, in addition to his tombstone, the church itself has a clock which he presented to it on his 64th birthday. When the clock was examined in 1833, there was found within it a paper on which was written, "This is the gift of the Right Honourable Chief Justice Hale to the Parish of Alderley. John Mason, Bristol, fecit 1 November 1673".[28] And in the secluded garden of the Middle Temple there is an old catalpa tree said to have been planted by Hale. On the lawn is a large table sun-dial, elaborately gilded and embellished.

According to Sir William Holdsworth, Coke stands midway between the medieval and the modern law whereas Hale is the first of our great modern common lawyers. "He possessed", he says, "a judicial impartiality which Coke never possessed, even when he was dealing with matters of public law. This impartiality was not shown by any other lawyer of his day, or by the post-Revolution lawyers who, as a general rule, adopted without criticism the legal and historical view upon controverted points of public law which the Revolution had caused to prevail".[29] This is largely true but Coke had qualities to which Hale could not aspire including not only his desire but his breathtaking efforts to ensure that judges were independent of the Crown. Nevertheless, even today some of Hale's work in his *History of the Pleas of the Crown* is cited in the higher courts to confirm difficult decisions in trials. And his commitment to the rule of law as it was understood in his day was total.

---

28. James McMullen Rigg. (1975) *Dictionary of National Biography*.
29. Sir William Holdsworth. (1966) *Some Makers of English Law*. Cambridge, Cambridge University Press, pp. 144-45.

CHAPTER 4

MAGNA CARTA AND HABEAS CORPUS

Magna Carta and Sir Edward Coke

Although there were community-based hundred courts and shire courts in Anglo-Saxon times, *Magna Carta* is probably the first meaningful recognition of the rule of law in England. As indicated earlier, chapters 39 and 40 as set out at its original signing in 1215 were as follows:

> 39. No free man shall be seized or imprisoned, or stripped of his rights or possessions, or outlawed or exiled, or deprived of his standing in any other way, nor will we proceed with force against him, or send others to do so, except by the lawful judgement of his equals or by the law of the land.
>
> 40. To no one will we sell to no one deny or delay right or justice.[1]

These were, of course, rights extracted from King John by his barons for their own benefit but the Great Charter, as it was then known, was expressed in general terms for all free men and in time it became a benchmark for all the citizens of Great Britain. Even at its signing it included the right to trial by one's peers and a precursor of *habeas corpus* and is a succinct outline of the fundamental basis of the rule of law.

In the early seventeenth century Coke dealt with *Magna Carta* in his *Second Institute*.[2] The Great Charter was sealed by a reluctant King John at Runnymede as a consequence of his disastrous foreign policy and financial administration. It was intended to prevent royal abuses of power. John soon persuaded the Pope to declare it invalid but subsequent monarchs were called upon to solemnly confirm it on no less than 37 different occasions.

---

1. Henry Marsh. (1971) *Documents of Liberty*. Newton Abbot, David and Charles (Publishers) Limited, p. 46.
2. Sir Edward Coke. (1779) 2 *Institutes of the Laws of England*. London, E. & R. Brooke.

Its guardian has been Parliament whose eventual triumph over the Crown was made possible by the revolutionary clause 12 which provides that, "No scutage or aid may be levied in our kingdom without its general consent ....". After the victory of Simon de Montfort against the Crown in 1264 this came to mean that the King was dependent on the Commons, who represented the kingdom, for an important part of his income. Coke chose to deal in the *Second Institute* with the third Great Charter, that of Henry III (1225) which he set out in full with his own annotations.

As we have seen, after being Attorney-General for Queen Elizabeth, Coke became Chief Justice during the reign of James I. He subsequently became a leader in the House of Commons against Charles I and used *Magna Carta* as a weapon against the authoritarian rule of the Stuart King. At the same time he had a profound influence upon the colonists in America where the English common law and Coke himself were held in high regard. Young colonists, and future Presidents, such as Thomas Jefferson and John Adams absorbed the Great Charter and the English common law from their acknowledged interpretation of them in the works of Coke.

Due Process of Law

Under due process of law a government is obliged to respect the legal rights of all its citizens. It means the system of rights and procedures, including adversariality, which allows the individual to confront the state on a level of equality and fairness. It also means that like any citizen the government itself is subject to the law of the land and the individual must be protected from infringement of his rights by the state. In other words, no person is to be deprived of life, liberty, property or other human rights unless decided upon in open court with an impartial jury at a hearing at which he or she has appeared and, if he or she so requests, has been represented. The concept is based upon basic fairness. As construed by the courts in the United States it includes the need to notify a defendant of the charges against him, an opportunity for him or her to be heard in their defence and that the tribunal is impartial. This is, of course, also the situation in the United Kingdom.

Nevertheless, many people consider that due process of law is a concept that operates mainly in the United States and appears to have little meaning in the United Kingdom. But, the meaning given to it above is clearly operating in the UK. Moreover, in fact, like much else to do with liberty its origins lie with the *Magna Carta* and with Sir Edward Coke in the seventeenth century.

As mentioned earlier, in clause 39 of *Magna Carta* the King promised that, "No free man shall be seized or imprisoned, or stripped of his rights or possessions, or outlawed or exiled, or deprived of his standing in any other way, nor will we proceed with force against him, or send others to do so, except by the lawful judgment of his equals or by the law of the land". This was meant to prevent the use of the courts to oppress the enemies of the King and it foretold the principle of the right to trial by jury.[3]

Clause 61 then provided for the barons to elect 25 of their number to guarantee the liberties of the Great Charter and by majority vote to decide upon redress if the King breached its terms or offended in any respect against any man.[4] This clause was intended to secure the good behaviour of the King and maintain the Charter. It involved aspects of the rule of law with the monarch subject to the law of the land and being limited as to how he or she could change that law. It was a revolution in the manner in which kings had ruled previously although its enforcement took a long time to be firmly secured in the reigns of the early Stuarts in the seventeenth century.

At King John's request, the Pope declared that the King was not bound by the Charter but the phrase "due process of law" appeared in a statutory version in 1354 in the reign of Edward III. This confirmed that, "No man of what state or condition he be, shall be put out of his lands or tenements nor taken, nor disinherited, nor put to death, without he be brought to answer by due process of law".[5]

According to Coke, the words, "the law of the land" in clause 39 of *Magna Carta* meant the same as "by due process of law". For him, he wrote in his *Second Institute,* it had constitutional significance in providing that

---

3. Henry Marsh. *Documents of Liberty from earliest times to universal suffrage, Op. cit.* p. 46.
4. *Ibid.* pp. 49-50.
5. 28 Edw. 3, c.3.

liberty and property were not to be interfered with without due process of the common law.⁶ This, in turn, led to the development of the writ of *habeas corpus* in the struggle of the common law courts against Chancery and the prerogative courts in Coke's day when, as part of protecting the liberty of the subject, the writ was widely used to free persons committed to prison by the Council. *Magna Carta's* prohibition of an arrest without due process of law was interpreted to mean due process of the common law in order to to show that arrests by order of the King and Council were illegal. This is how it was interpreted for a time in England and it was to sink deeply into thinking in the United States where the Bill of Rights provides that "No person shall be ... deprived of life, liberty or property, without due process of law".

Despite these historical origins, however, the phrase has never taken deep root in English legal language although it is clearly part of what we understand by the rule of law. Particularly as:

> Due process of law implies the right of the person affected thereby to be present before the tribunal which pronounces judgement upon the question of life, liberty, or property, in its most comprehensive sense; to be heard by testimony or otherwise, and to have the right of controverting, by proof, every material fact which bears on the question of right in the matter involved. If any question of fact or liability be conclusively presumed against him, this is not due process of law.⁷

And another commentator has spoken of a global, silent revolution, largely unremarked, which has accelerated in the last decades to precipitous speed and is one of the most important changes in our generation. "It has", he says, "huge implications for our whole culture and for our liberties and the prospect of equality and it can best be described as a global revolution in *Due Process*".⁸ He argues that due process is important because you can have all the enacted human rights imaginable but without procedures to make them bite it does not mean a thing. "In 1936, for example, Stalin enacted a wonderful constitution, described at the time a 'the most democratic the world has ever seen'. It probably was. But without good procedure it did not

---

6. Sir Edward Coke. *2 Institutes of the Laws of England, Op. cit.* pp. 50-51.
7. Black's Law Dictionary, 6th edition, p. 500.
8. Richard Vogler. (2006) *Criminal Justice and Due Process: A Global Revolution?* Unpublished Lecture in Lewes, Sussex.

stop him arresting 1.5 million people without charge during the Great Terror of the same year and executing an estimated 700,000 without trial".[9] By due process Vogler says he means a system of rights and procedures which allows the individual to confront the state on a level of equality and fairness and that includes adversariality.

In the United Kingdom, Parliament is supreme and can protect (or restrict) trial by jury, freedom of the press and liberty of conscience without a Supreme Court being able to limit its power. Although at the present time the judiciary is exercising its muscles against the executive more openly than in the past with the use of judicial review.[10] And some authoritative voices are questioning whether sovereignty is incompatible with the rule of law.[11]

In the United States a different view prevails based to some extent on the early views of Coke on this question. In England in 1610 Coke declared in *Bonham's Case*[12] that, "it appears in our books, that in many cases, the common law will control Acts of Parliament, and sometimes adjudge them to be utterly void".[13] But he changed his mind two years later in the case of *Rowles v. Mason*[14] and did not mention the Bonham issue in his *Institutes* where he finally accepted Parliament's overriding power. Nonetheless, the natural law principle of judicial appeal against statutes found fertile ground in the young United States, leading to the review role of the Supreme Court today with the concept of fundamental law to restrain both the executive and legislature alike and to disallow statutes if they conflict with the Constitution.

It is interesting in this context that in 1842 in Scotland the courts held that a statute was inoperative because the forms prescribed by the two Houses of Parliament at Westminster to be observed in the enactment of a Bill had not been followed exactly. The House of Lords found it necessary to tell the courts that that they were acting beyond their powers. In giving his judgment in the case Lord Campbell said:

---

9. *Ibid.*
10. See John Hostettler. (June 2004) "The Rule of Law v. Parliamentary Supremacy". *The Legal Executive Journal.* pp. 24-5.
11. Sir Francis Jacobs. *The Sovereignty of Law: The European Way.* (2007) Cambridge, Cambridge University Press. p. 5.
12. Coke. (1610) *Bonham's Case.* 8 Reports. p. 375.
13. *Ibid.* 111b.
14. 2 Brownlow. (1612) p. 198.

I cannot but express my surprise that such a notion should ever have prevailed. There is no foundation whatever for it. All that a court of justice can do is to look to the Parliament roll: if from that it should appear that a Bill has passed both houses and received the royal assent, no court of justice can inquire into the mode in which it was introduced into Parliament, nor what was done previous to its introduction, or what passed in Parliament during its progress in its various stages through both houses. I trust, therefore, that no such inquiry will again be entered upon in any court in Scotland, but that full effect will be given to every Act of Parliament, private as well as public, upon what appears to be the proper construction of its existing provisions.[15]

This, of course, is not the position taken in United States jurisprudence where due process is highly regarded as meaning the government must respect a person's legal rights according to law. Government is considered to be subservient to the law of the land in addition to legislating the law. Even enacted law can be held to be unconstitutional and invalid by the Supreme Court. It is a concept that has no place in modern British legal theory.

Habeas Corpus

The right to *habeas corpus* is to be found in *Magna Carta* but it is believed to pre-date 1215. Although Sir William Blackstone in his *Commentaries on the Laws of England,* declared that the first use of *habeas corpus* was in 1305, similar writs were in use in the twelve century and some believe its origins are to be found in Anglo-Saxon dooms. However, *Magna Carta* provides for the courts to seek out the whereabouts of a prisoner and disallows the selling or the delay of justice. Today, *habeas corpus* is a writ to safeguard the liberty of the individual. It requires a person detained by the authorities be brought before the High Court in order that the legality of the detention may be examined. It is a flexible and wide-ranging remedy and the court may order the immediate release of a person held unlawfully.

In 1627, Charles I attempted to raise forced loans without the consent of Parliament. For refusing to pay some seventy wealthy men, including Sir Thomas Wentworth, were arbitrarily jailed. Five complained that they had

---

15. John Hostettler. "The Rule of Law v. Parliamentary Supremacy". Op. *cit.*, pp. 24-25.

been committed without cause shown and applied to the King's Bench for *habeas corpus* in what became known as the *Case of the Five Knights*.[16] Lawyers for the knights, including John Selden, argued that although the King might imprison subjects he must, by *Magna Carta,* show cause for doing so. For the Crown the talented Attorney-General, Sir Robert Heath, afterwards Chief Justice of the Common Pleas, declared that reason of state was sufficient and, even if men were innocent, if their liberty would be dangerous to the state they should be detained in prison until the King was ready to bring them to trial.

And the court decided that if no cause were given by the King the prisoners could not be freed as the offence was probably too dangerous for public discussion. However, once collection of the loan was completed the men were released but their imprisonment had caused a number of MPs, including Coke, to call for the implementation of *Magna Carta*. Coke then seized the opportunity to extend the demand to a wider call for liberty. In doing so he prepared Resolutions which, fifty-two years later, were to form the foundation of the Habeas Corpus Act 1679.

Later in 1627, Charles, requiring new subsidies, was obliged to call a fresh Parliament. He endeavoured to claim extensive rights for the Crown and in response the fiery Cornish knight, Sir John Eliot, declared to the Commons that they faced the questioning of the rights that had made their fathers free men in a manner that would give leave to the Crown to annihilate or decline any Act of Parliament. Coke added that Bracton had said that any Act against the Great Charter was void. The fundamental law could not be annulled by statute.

It was in 1679 that Parliament enacted the Habeas Corpus Act[17] *to* define and strengthen the prerogative writ. The statute first recited that *Magna Carta* should be fully operated. It further provided that:

1. No freeman is to be committed or detained in prison, or otherwise restrained by command of the King or the Privy Council or any other, unless some lawful cause be shown.

---
16. *Darnell's Case.* Cobbett's *State Trials.* (1809-1828) London, R. Bagshaw. vol. iii. col. 1.
17. 31 Cha. 2. c. 2.

2. The writ of *habeas corpus* cannot be denied, but should be granted to every man who is committed or detained in prison or otherwise restrained by the command of the King, the Privy Council or any other.
3. Any freeman so committed or detained in prison without cause being stated should be entitled to bail or be freed.

It was also confirmed that no tax or loan was to be levied without the consent of Parliament, and no one was to be compelled to receive soldiers into his house against his will.[18]

Coke and others presented the Resolutions to the House of Lords for its approval with Coke citing seven statutes and thirty-one precedents to support their case. "Imprisonment in law", he told their Lordships, "is a civil death" with the prisoner less than a bondsman or villain. "The greatest inheritance a man hath is the liberty of his person …". The law, he said, would never have given the many remedies he had set out if the freemen of England might have been imprisoned at will and pleasure.[19] The peers rejected the Resolutions and put forward alternatives that supported the King. Coke attacked them bitterly. *Magna Carta*, he said, was not a matter of the King's grace but the subject's right and the common law of the land. Reason of state lamed the Charter. In the event, the King refused to accept the Resolutions saying the Commons should trust his word. Coke then repeated to the House of Lords that the greatest inheritance that a man had, "is the liberty of his person, for all others are accessory to it".

Although the Bill appears to have passed in the House of Lords by an error in the counting of the votes, the statute guaranteed the right to *habeas corpus* in law and severely reduced the powers of the Crown to imprison without trial.

---

18. *Parliamentary History*. (1679) vol. ii. p. 259.
19. *Ibid.* pp. 266-71.

CHAPTER 5

CESARE BECCARIA

Unsung Genius

How many people in England today have heard of Cesare Beccaria? Relatively few, I imagine. And the same could have been said of him in Europe before 1764 when, at the age of twenty-six, he wrote his short book entitled, *On Crimes and Punishments* (*Dei Delitti e delle Pene* in its original Italian). Yet a year later his fame was world-wide because of the sheer genius of the book. Why then is he so little known today? The answer lies in the phenomenal success his book had when first published and the fact that his achievements have now become part of the fabric of our lives. As a consequence, we take freedom from cruel criminal laws for granted and give little thought to how such freedom was brought about. But those achievements, encapsulated in the concepts of human rights and the rule of law, are now in some instances under threat in many parts of the globe including the United Kingdom. Which makes a fresh study of the work of Beccaria relevant in the modern world.

Inquisitorial Trial

In the early eighteenth century the state of the criminal law in England was bleak. But in continental Europe the situation was far worse. Gallows were a regular feature of the landscape, branding and mutilation were common as punishments and men were tortuously broken on the wheel. Secret accusations were endemic in France, Italy, Russia and many other countries. Torture to extract confessions was integral to the penal code and punishments, which were often determined behind closed doors at the whim of judges and magistrates who were demonstrably unsuited to the role, were unbelievably harsh. Persons accused of crimes were presumed guilty and the judiciary was not independent but formed part of the executive power, with judges acting as prosecutors on behalf of the all-pervading state. Equality before the law was an unknown concept and a mere accusation was often accepted by the courts as *prima facie* evidence of guilt.

Essentially, the rule of law was disregarded in favour of judicial ferocity and cruelty. Indeed, the rule of law was not only unrecognised, no effort was made to understand it. When we consider the precepts of the rule of law we find they were all broken under the inquisitorial system. For a person to be tried, convicted and executed it was not necessary to be in breach of any law. The courts were not ordinary courts of law and there was no equality before them for the different ranks in society. Civil liberties were infringed at will, there was no *habeas corpus* or effective jury trial and men of position could obtain from the Crown *lettres de cachet* by which people could be seized and imprisoned indefinitely without ever being charged or brought before a court. In France, alongside economic distress and poverty, all this and the despair it caused led finally to the storming of the Bastille and the French Revolution.

In this pitiless milieu the Italian Count Cesara Beccaria set out to challenge the status quo. He believed in the social contract theory that men are naturally independent but originally joined themselves into society. Weary of living in a continual state of war, with liberty of little value, they sacrificed part of their independence to enjoy the remainder in peace and security. And to defend themselves from usurpation by some despotic individuals they accepted the need for punishments. But the reality had nothing in common with the original idea. Passions opposed to the general good, he said, could not be restrained for any length of time merely by the power of eloquence or truth. Hence he recognised a need for punishments but he firmly believed that they should never be excessive or harsh – as they so often were in his day – and should serve the greatest public good. For Beccaria, the purpose of punishment was to assist in creating a better society.

Cri de Coeur

In Beccaria destiny made a strange choice. He was born in 1738, the eldest son of an aristocratic family in Milan, a city of 120,000 people in Lombardy. Shy to a painful degree he had no legal training or experience beyond obtaining a law degree. Yet at the age of 26 years he produced a book, *On Crimes and Punishments,* that was to shatter the foundations of criminal law systems throughout Europe. It was to make a major contribution to the cause of humanity and justice in countries that included the Russia of Catherine the Great, the Prussia of Frederick II, the Austria-Hungary of Maria Theresa as well as France, Italy and Sweden. It was not the first protest against the bleak inhumanity of the criminal law, nor was it merely a plea for some change. Rather, was it a *cri de coeur* for a complete reform of the criminal law which gave rise to an intellectual movement for a more rational and enlightened society.

The success of the book was explained by Marcello Maestro who wrote that, "The great merit of Beccaria's book – and this explains its great success and the practical impact that it would soon have in many countries – lies in the fact that for the first time the principles of a penal reform were expressed in a systematic and concise way, and the rights of humanity were defended in the clearest terms, with the most logical arguments.[1]

Watershed

On Crimes and Punishments was published in Livorno on 12 April 1764, at roughly the same time as adversary trial was beginning to emerge in England. Together the book and adversary trial raised the issues of human rights for prisoners and brought the rule of law to the forefront. They created a watershed in the history of the rule of law and criminal justice, not only in continental Europe and England but across the globe. Gradually, individuals were to acquire opportunities for defence that had been denied them

---

1. Marcello Maestro. (1973) *Cesare Beccaria and the Origins of Penal Reform.* Philadelphia, Temple University Press, p. 34.

for centuries and almost immediately punishments were to be made more humane for those found guilty of criminal acts.

In the age of enlightenment Beccaria stands out for his deep humanity and belief in human reason which inspired his attempt to perfect criminal law and procedure. His book was the first work that heralded a more humane spirit of criminal legislation. The effects of his attacks on the terrors underpinning the system of criminal justice were both immediate and influential in continental Europe. This included revolutionary France, until later when the introduction of the Napoleonic Code largely re-instated the medieval type *Code Louis* of 1670. In a significant contribution to the rule of law, Beccaria's native Lombardy, Portugal, Austria, Russia and France all abolished torture and reformed their criminal justice systems as a direct result of the potency of his onslaughts.

Declaration of the Rights of Man and of the Citizen

To kick-start this process, on 14 July 1789 Parisians attacked the Bastille, the feared symbolic institution of the French criminal justice system. Fewer than six weeks later, the French Declaration of the Rights of Man and the Citizen was approved by the French National Assembly on 26 August. The Declaration, which sets out the rule of law, was largely the work of the Marquis de Lafayette after consulting with Thomas Jefferson in Paris where he was then American Minister to France. In its first article it declares that "men are born and remain free and equal in rights". Liberty, it continues, consists in the freedom to do everything which injures no one else and no one shall be punished except by virtue of a law enacted before the offence and legally applied.

Law, says article 5, could only prohibit such actions as are hurtful to society. Nothing may be prevented which is not forbidden by law, and no one may be forced to do anything not provided for by law. By article 7, "No person shall be accused, arrested or imprisoned except in the cases and according to the forms prescribed by law". Article 8 provides that the only punishments should be those that are strictly and obviously necessary, and no one should suffer punishment unless it is legally inflicted in virtue of a law passed before the commission of the offence.

Whilst, in an English assize court in 1791 William Garrow was the first lawyer to express clearly the presumption of innocence[2] the Declaration provides, in article 9, that as all persons are held to be innocent until found guilty. If arrest is considered indispensible, all harshness not essential to securing the prisoner's person should be severely repressed by law. Opinions and religious beliefs were to be sacrosanct provided they did not disturb public order and the free communication of ideas was guaranteed. Clearly it was not only to Jefferson that Lafayette owed thanks but also to Beccaria.

As part of the fabric of the rule of law, Beccaria held that the law must be clear and precise, not arbitrary. Trial by a person's peers was essential, secret accusations should be outlawed, proof of a crime should be perfect and laws should be passed by legislation and should not be created by judges. The law, not punishments, should be feared since fear of punishment led to a great deal of crime. Indeed, it was better to prevent crimes than to punish them. In fact, Beccaria's book has shaped much of the modern system of criminology.

Torture

Secret accusations and torture, which are outlawed by the rule of law, were endemic in continental Europe in Beccaria's day. They were essential elements of the inquisitorial system. Leading jurists not only supported them but wrote about how best to accomplish them. The Roman Catholic Church argued that torture was a mercy to the criminal since it purged him in death from the sin of falsehood. This, said Beccaria, was "a ridiculous motive for torture which should not be tolerated". And what if the prisoner were not guilty? There was no such thing as an open trial and often there was no trial at all. In France, *Lettres de cachet* were issued by monarchs to have persons arrested and held in dungeons indefinitely without charge or trial. Sometimes they were handed out with the name of the person to be arrested left

---

2. OBP Online. (www.oldbaileyonline.org, 20 July 2010) 14 September 1791. Trial of George Dingler for Murder. Ref: t17910914-1.

blank to be filled in by the person receiving the *lettre*. Tortures to obtain confessions of guilt were horrendous and widespread. Beccaria argued that society should not deprive a man of its protection until it had been proved that he had committed a crime and, even then, torture should not be used. A man could not be called guilty, he said, until he had been sentenced by a court so what right had a judge to inflict punishment on a citizen whilst his guilt or innocence remained in doubt? Who, he asked, could possibly defend himself against false accusations which were supported by tyranny's impenetrable shield of secrecy?

A man, he said, was either guilty or not guilty. If proved to be guilty he should be punished according to the law and torture became useless, since his confession was unnecessary. If he was not guilty, an innocent man was tortured to no purpose. He deplored the idea that pain was the crucible of truth, as if the test of it "lay in the muscles and sinews of an unfortunate wretch".

A curious consequence that flowed naturally from the use of torture, he exclaimed, was that an innocent man was placed in a worse condition than a guilty one. If both were tortured the former had every alternative against him. For either he confessed the crime and was condemned or he was declared innocent having suffered an undeserved punishment. But the guilty man had one chance in his favour, since, if he resisted the torture firmly and was acquitted, he had exchanged a greater penalty for a smaller one. Therefore, whilst an innocent man could only lose by torture, one who is guilty might gain by it.

Shortly after Beccaria's book was published its message on torture spread like wildfire across Europe and so powerful were its words that torture was abolished in all the major countries.

Capital Punishment

By Beccaria's time the death penalty was deep-rooted in continental Europe's history with appalling methods of execution including the horrendous breaking on the wheel. In England, the "Bloody Code" meant death on the scaffold for over 200 crimes, many of them trivial such as theft of cash or an article of clothing or food with a value of a shilling. For high treason the penalty was merciless. A man found guilty was drawn behind a cart to the place of execution, hanged and cut down whilst still alive, disembowelled and castrated, with his intestines burnt before his eyes and finally decapitated with the remainder of his body cut into quarters. Women found guilty of treason were burnt at the stake after being tarred, although in many cases the executioner managed to strangle them before they were engulfed by the flames of the fire.

Although others had opposed the death penalty, Beccaria was the first to mount an original and sustained critique of its use. He denied that the penalty could be justified in any circumstances believing that it did not act as a deterrent and that it was both immoral and useless. Furthermore, the death penalty was not only cruel and excessive, it failed to either reduce of effectively punish crime. And, imprisonment was a stronger deterrent since hanging was transient.

He was adamant that a man should not be killed by the authority of the law. What kind of right can that be, he asked, which men claim for the slaughter of their fellow-beings? What man ever wished to leave to others the option of killing him? The death penalty was not right. It was not only immoral, it was useless and did not deter. It was itself a barbarous act of violence and an injustice since it rendered an act legitimate in payment for an equivalent act of violence. Moreover, it was harmful to society in reducing sensitivity to human suffering. Countries and times most atrocious for the severity of punishments, he declared, were always those in which the most atrocious crimes were committed; for the hand of the legislator and that of the assassin were directed by the same spirit of ferocity.[3]

Again, Beccaria's ideas were swiftly adopted across Europe. For instance, in Russia, Catherine I abolished both the gallows and the wheel. Catherine II went further in desiring to establish a reformed and uniform penal code and asked Beccaria to go to Russia and introduce the reforms in person. In Tuscany and Rome the death penalty was abolished and in France the Revolution put an end to it being used for over one hundred different offences.

---

3. C. Beccaria. (1775) *An Essay on Crimes and Punishments with a Commentary Attributed to Monsieur De Voltaire. Translated from the French.* 4th edn. London, F. Newbery, p. 99.

In England where there was no torture and some elements of the rule of law, it took longer, but by 1837 execution on the gallows was confined to cases of murder and treason.

Attacks on Beccaria

Outside of England there was venomous opposition to Beccaria from the Roman Catholic Church and some lawyers. The Inquisition forbade the use of Beccaria's book under pain of death and placed it on the Index in 1766. Beccaria was described as a madman, and a stupid imposter full of poisonous bitterness. A lawyer of Provence joined in the attempted character assassination saying Beccaria was attempting to overturn laws received by the greater part of all civilizations.[4] And an advocate to the Parliament of Paris attacked Beccaria, asking, "What can be thought of an author who presumes to establish his system on the *débris* of all hitherto accepted notions who to accredit it condemns all civilized nations, and who spares neither systems of law, nor magistrates, nor lawyers".

"Electrical Effect"

As we shall see Beccaria, was praised by English law reformers and in America by Thomas Jefferson. Another American President who read and absorbed Beccaria's treatise was John Adams. In 1770, long before he became President, Adams defended British soldiers charged in connection with the "Boston Massacre". In his opening words to the jury, he said "I am for the prisoners at the bar, and shall apologise for it only in the words of the marquis Beccaria: "If I can but be the instrument of preserving one life, his blessing and tears of transport shall be a sufficient consolation to me for the contempt of all mankind".[5] It is interesting that John Adams, a Founding Father of

---

4. J. A. Farrer. (1880) *Crimes and Punishments including a new translation of Beccaria's Dei Delitti e Delle Pene.* London, Chatto & Windus p. 18.
5. Frederic Kidder. (1870) *History of the Boston Massacre.* Albany, New York. p. 232.

the United States of America and its second President, used this sentiment from Beccaria and as John Quincey Adams, his grandson and sixth President, was later to recall, "the electrical effect produced upon the jury, and upon the immense and excited auditory, by the first sentence with which he opened his defense, which was a citation from the then recently published work of Beccaria".[6]

The so-called massacre arose from a number of youths snowballing a party of redcoats. Some soldiers, without orders, fired at the youths, killing three outright and wounding others, two of whom died later. Some of the men were put on trial but there was no conclusive evidence that an order to fire had been given, or who fired the shots, with the result that all were acquitted. The passage from Beccaria, spoken with passion by John Adams, may also have had a powerful effect on the jury. Clearly Adams' grandson thought so. And also clear is that the soldiers benefitted from the rule of law in a city that would have little sympathy for them.

Beccaria dealt with all aspects of penal laws, always arguing for the spirit of the rule of law. And he concluded his book with a striking sentence that

> In order that every punishment may not be an act of violence, committed by one man or by many against a single individual it ought to be above all things public, speedy, necessary, the least possible in the given circumstances, proportioned to its crime, dictated by the laws.[7]

Death

Beccaria died suddenly of apoplexy at his home on 28 November 1794 at the age of 57. He was survived by his daughter, Giulia, and his son Giulio. He had enjoyed a life of solitude and was largely unmourned at the time. Milan is famed for its beautiful cathedral, Leonardo da Vinci's "Last Supper" and La Scala Opera House. It also now has two statues of Beccaria but

---

6. Charles Francis Adams. (1856) *The Works of John Adams, second President of the United States, with a life of the author, notes and illustrations.* Boston, Little Brown. vol. ii. pp. 238-9.
7. J.A. Farrer. *Crimes and Punishments including a new translation of Beccaria's Dei Delitti e Delle Pene, Op. cit.* p. 251.

that is all. In a sense this arises from the fact that he was indifferent to honours and, indeed, society. When the King of Naples called upon him at his home on two occasions he made sure he was out. His extreme shyness, which continued throughout his life, caused untold difficulties but as a writer he exhibited great moral courage in the land which established the Inquisition and this shone through his work which is itself his lasting epitaph. It had an important input to the United States Constitution, the Bill of Rights and our own criminal justice system.

Law reformers Jefferson, Bentham, Romilly and the Criminal Law Commissioners all paid fulsome tributes to Beccaria and all used his arguments in their own efforts to give meaning and life to the concept of the rule of law. In truth, Beccaria was perhaps the greatest exponent of the rule of law in history.[8]

Current Issues

Today, there are again sharp disagreements on the purposes of punishment and the function of prisons. In many parts of the world, including as a consequence of recent experiences in the United States, the use of capital punishment and forms of torture is again exciting the minds and passions of many people. Beccaria pointed the way with his fervent opposition to arbitrary rule, cruelty and intolerance and his book is a powerful stimulus in helping to resolve current issued in criminal law and making clear the proper role of the criminal justice system. It reflects Beccaria's "sincere sympathy for the most unfortunate and unjustly treated sections of humanity" and his "earnest desire to see the triumph of real justice in a more civilized society".[9]

The perception and reasoning of Beccaria about the need for humanity in the criminal law and the function of the rule of law as a binding force in society show the genius of a book that still has many lessons for the lawyers, criminologists, and, indeed, many people of twenty-first century Britain.

---

8. For more on Beccaria see John Hostettler. (2010) *Cesare Beccaria: The Genius of 'On Crimes and Punishments'*. Hook, Hampshire, Waterside Press.
9. Marcello Maestro. *Cesare Beccaria and the Origins of Penal Reform. Op. cit.* p. 35.

At a time when civil liberties are being threatened by the belief of men with power, such as former President George W. Bush who considers that waterboarding is no torture, and the former Prime Minister, Tony Blair, who has said that it is a dangerous misjudgment to put civil liberties before anti-terrorist laws, it is to be profoundly hoped that the rule of law and human rights will prevail.

Champions of the Rule of Law

CHAPTER 6

THOMAS JEFFERSON

Family and Youth

Thomas Jefferson, the author of the American Declaration of Independence, was born on 13 April 1743 at Shadwell, Virginia. His father, Peter, was a tobacco planter and surveyor who mapped the Northern Wilderness. His mother, Jan Randolph, was a member of one of Virginia's most prominent families of wealthy English and Scottish gentry. Thomas was the third of ten children, two of whom died in childhood. At 25 he married Martha Skelton and they were happily married until she died ten years later. During that time they had six children but, as often occurred at the time, only two of them reached adulthood.

In 1752 Jefferson started at a local school and at the age of nine was studying Latin, Greek and French. His elder sister Jane taught him to read and he learned to play the violin. After his father died in 1757, leaving him some 5,000 acres of land and dozens of slaves, he was taught the classics, history and science by James Maury. Eight years later, when he was 16, he entered the College of William and Mary in Williamsburg and studied philosophy, metaphysics and mathematics. He toiled hard – it is said he frequently studied for fifteen hours a day – and became proficient in languages, although, at this stage, he was not involved with legal studies. It was here he acquired his great love of wine. In 1762 he graduated with high honours.

Profession of Law

Although he had not studied law at college, and he still preferred science and the arts, at the age of twenty Jefferson made law his chosen profession in order to give service in society. In accordance with usual practice he commenced an apprenticeship in a lawyer's office but soon struck out on a hard-working course of self-study. In all, he spent five years in reading law with William and Mary law professor and jurist George Wythe, who made him an Enlightenment figure. And, in 1767, at the age of 24 he was admitted to the Bar of the General Court in colonial Williamsburg with a determination to use the law in aid of an anti-British revolutionary government. Nevertheless, he practised as counsel in hundreds of cases in the General Court which consisted of the colony's Governor and Council and had both original and appellate jurisdiction in criminal and civil cases. Jefferson also undertook cases in the inferior county courts for lower fees which were fixed by law. He seems to have been at ease in court with an appealing manner although he was not an outstanding orator. His work in the law did, however, lay the groundwork for his political life.

At the time in Virginia there were no law schools, few law books and no American law reports. Indeed, there was no clearly defined set of colonial laws. Nevertheless, he commenced to study the works of Sir Edward Coke which must have given him a good grounding in both the common law and constitutional law despite his calling Coke "an old dull scoundrel". He did, however, come in time to admire this champion of English rights and liberties who had a considerable effect upon the American Founding Fathers.

In addition to his practice as a barrister, in 1769 Jefferson became the representative of the county of Albemarle in the Virginia House of Burgesses where he met George Washington and where he was in office until 1776. And, in 1774 he wrote a set of resolutions against the Coercive Acts passed at Westminster which were soon expanded into his first brilliant published treatise, *A Summary View of the Rights of British America.* In this he made the then novel suggestion that the colonists had the right to govern themselves and that the Westminster Parliament had no right to legislate for the colonies. Like Coke, he stressed both individual rights and liberty and the sovereignty of the nation. In doing so he gave a structure to the rising demand for independence in the American colonies. And the rule of law was at the core of all he wrote. For Jefferson, law was not only an essential cement for the fabric of society, it was truly ennobling.

He believed that the rule of law had its origins in Anglo-Saxon England, particularly with the laws of King Alfred the Great. The preamble to Alfred's book of laws had contained a translation of the ten commandments into

English, numerous passages from the book of Exodus and a brief account of apolistic history. Further, Alfred endeavoured to ensure that there was not to be one law for the rich and another for the poor. Jefferson firmly considered that Alfred's dooms, as they were known, formed the basis of Coke's works. He also agreed with Sir Matthew Hale and others that Christianity was part of the law of England despite this being difficult to prove. Jefferson used the myth about Saxon law against the mother country and argued that it was destroyed by the imposition of the "Norman Yoke" which commenced with the rule and laws of William the Conqueror and the Normans. It had taken the English Civil War to destroy the "Norman Yoke" and Jefferson welcomed with open arms the emerging rule of law that Britain then offered.

Soon after the outbreak of the American War of Independence, in June 1775, Jefferson was a delegate from Virginia to the Second Continental Congress. Whilst there he desired to return to Virginia to help write that state's Constitution. Instead, a year later he was appointed to a five-man committee to write the first draft of a declaration to accompany a resolution of the independence of the colonies following the dissolution of the union with Great Britain on 7 June 1776. Jefferson completed his draft using as a guide his own proposals for a Declaration of Rights for Virginia and other sources. He wrote a stirring statement setting out the right of the colonists to rebel against the British government and establish their own based upon the principle he made familiar that all men are created equal and have the inalienable rights to life, liberty and the pursuit of happiness. After some revisions were made by others it was presented to Congress and on 4 July 1776 the Declaration of Independence was approved.

It set out the ideas of natural rights that would form the basis of constitutional government. But only in 1788 was the United States Constitution ratified as the basic law of the United States. It promised a jury for all trials except impeachment, and later Amendments added the right to a speedy trial, the right for a defendant to obtain witnesses and face those accusing him and to have the assistance of counsel in his defence. This involved acceptance of the principles of the common law including adversary trial. Jefferson had played the dominant role in writing the Declaration and this was his finest hour.

And, in September 1776 he had managed to return to Virginia where he was elected to the House of Delegates. Here he set out to reform Virginia's system of law and within three years he had drafted 126 Bills. One of these was to rid the state of the death penalty for all crimes other than murder and treason but it was defeated.

From 1 June 1779 to 3 June 1781 he was the second Governor of Virginia having been preceded by Patrick Henry. He was President of the United States from 4 March 1801 with Aaron Burr as Vice-President. He is the only president to have served two full terms without vetoing a single Bill of Congress.

Virginia

When the American War of Independence had begun in the mid-1770s there were in Pennsylvania nearly 20 capital crimes but by 1794, largely as a result of Beccaria's influence, only murder in the first degree led to the gallows. Indeed, Jefferson read Beccaria's treatise in the original Italian and copied long passages into his commonplace book.[1] This contained 26 extracts from Beccaria in Italian, all long passages cited in Jefferson's own handwriting.[2] However, even after the creation of the United States, in Jefferson's native Virginia English criminal law still reigned with offenders variously hanged, whipped, pilloried, branded and dismembered. But Jefferson was opposed to capital punishment for all crimes except treason and wilful murder and, in 1785, he introduced into the Virginia legislature a clumsily worded but important Bill for Proportioning Crimes and Punishments in Cases heretofore Capital, with Beccaria's *On Crimes and Punishments* mentioned in four footnotes. He explained to Wythe, "In style I have aimed at accuracy, brevity and simplicity… Indeed, I wished to exhibit a sample of reformation in the barbarous style into which modern statutes have degenerated from their ancient simplicity".[3] In some respects the Bill was flawed and it

---

1. Merrill D. Peterson. (1970) *Thomas Jefferson & the new nation.* New York, Oxford University Press. p. 124.
2. Marcello Maestro. (1973) *Cesare Beccaria and the Origins of Penal Reform.* Philadelphia, Temple University Press. p. 141.
3. Merrill D. Peterson. *Thomas Jefferson & the new nation. Op. cit.* p. 125.

was eventually defeated by a single vote in December 1786. It was, however, later approved when submitted again in 1796.

It is noteworthy that in the Bill Jefferson set out three cardinal principles which he derived from Beccaria. First, since punishment is an evil in itself, it is justified only so far as it produces greater happiness through the reformation of the criminal and the future prevention of crime. Secondly, punishments more severe than necessary to prevent crimes defeat their object by "engaging the benevolence of mankind to withhold prosecutions, to smother testimony, or to listen to it with bias ...". Thirdly, crimes are more effectively prevented by the certainty than by the severity of punishment. As a consequence, certain penalties should be clearly associated with certain crimes and justice should be swift and sure, protected from judicial caprice and special dispensations of any kind. As he remarked, "Let mercy be the character of the law-giver, but let the judge be a mere machine".[4]

Nevertheless, he was sometimes at cross-purposes with his own beliefs. In Virginia the practices of gouging out of eyes and the biting off of ears were endemic. One observer recorded, "I have seen a fellow, reckoned a great adept in gouging who constantly kept the nails of both his thumbs and second fingers very long and pointed; nay, to prevent their breaking or splitting... he hardened [them] every evening in a candle". Considering which punishments would be appropriate for such crimes as rape, sodomy, maiming and disfiguring he wanted the punishment to be retaliation in kind, although his mind was repelled by the idea. And, forty years later he was puzzled to account for the sanction given to this "revolting principle"[5] However, it was a "principle" that Jeremy Bentham was also to embrace.

Jefferson and the Rule of Law

Jefferson's dedication to the rule of law is clear from his determination to secure an American Bill of Rights. As Alistair Cooke has written:

---

4. *Ibid.* p. 126.
5. *Ibid.* p. 127.

Champions of the Rule of Law

There might have been no workable Constitution, and no all-powerful Court, if the Founding Fathers had not listened, though rather late in the day, to an American who was not present in Philadelphia. He is the missing giant of the Constitutional Convention, Thomas Jefferson. He was in Paris as Minister to France, and he heard with alarm that George Mason had failed to impress on the Convention the vital need for a written bill of rights. He unceasingly nagged every influential man he knew until he got it. Looking around him in France, Jefferson was a daily witness to the old indignities and assaults on personal liberty that the Constitution had failed to prohibit. And he wrote home continually that it was not enough to presume the sanctity of those human rights whose violation was all too familiar to the Founding Fathers. You must, he wrote, "specify" those liberties and put them down on paper.[6]

Within four years, on 15 December 1791, ten amendments of the Constitution were ratified as the Bill of Rights. Six of them are crucial ingredients of the rule of law. They are:

1. The right of the people to be secure in their persons, houses, papers, and effects, against unreasonable searches and seizures, shall not be violated, and no Warrants shall issue, but upon probable cause, supported by Oath or affirmation, and particularly describing the place to be searched, and the persons or things to be seized.
2. No person shall be held to answer for a capital, or otherwise infamous crime, unless on a presentment or indictment of a Grand Jury, except in cases arising in the land or naval forces, or in the Militia, when in actual service in time of War or public danger; nor shall any person be subject for the same offence to be twice put in jeopardy of life or limb; nor shall be compelled in any criminal case to be a witness against himself, nor be deprived of life, liberty, or property, without due process of law; nor shall private property be taken for public use, without just compensation.
3. In all criminal prosecutions, the accused shall enjoy the right to a speedy and public trial, by an impartial jury of the State and district wherein the crime shall have been committed, which district shall have been previously ascertained by law, and to be informed of the nature

---

6. *Alistair Cooke's America.* (1973) London, British Broadcasting Corporation, p. 147.

and cause of the accusation; to be confronted with the witnesses against him; to have compulsory process for obtaining witnesses in his favour, and to have the Assistance of Counsel for his defence.
4. In Suits at common law, where the value in controversy shall exceed twenty dollars, the right of trial by jury shall be preserved, and no fact tried by a jury shall be otherwise re-examined in any Court of the United States, than according to the rules of the common law.
5. Excessive bail shall not be required, nor excessive fines imposed, nor cruel and unusual punishments inflicted.
6. The enumeration in the Constitution of certain rights shall not be construed to deny or disparage others retained by the people.

Trial by Jury

It is clear that by the right to trial by jury in the Bill of Rights, Jefferson intended to go beyond the position in England where the jury were never allowed to interpret the law – that was for the judge alone in all cases. Jefferson said in 1782, in his *Notes on the State of Virginia,* … "it is usual for the jurors to decide the fact, and to refer the law arising on it to the decision of the judges. But this division of the subject lies with their discretion only. And if the question relates to any point of public liberty, or if it be one of those in which the judges may be suspected of bias, the jury undertake to decide both law and fact". And, recommending trial by jury to the French in 1789, Jefferson wrote to Tom Paine, "I consider … [trial by jury] as the only anchor yet imagined by man, by which a government can be held to their principles of its constitution". He also supported the introduction of jury trial into the court of Chancery but this surprising innovative reform did not last.

Death

Jefferson and his wife Martha had five daughters and one son, who was stillborn. He died at the neoclassical mansion he had constructed known as Monticello, in Charlottesville, Virginia, surrounded by his family, on 4 July 1826, the fiftieth anniversary of the ratification of the American Declaration of Independence. He died a few hours before John Adams his friend and political rival who had both fought for independence for the American colonies. He is regarded by many as the greatest American who ever lived and the greatest United States President. And, in addition to all his great achievements as legislator, statesman and President, he is also remembered for his constant attachment to, and advocacy of, the rule of law.

CHAPTER 7

JEREMY BENTHAM

Science of Law

Jeremy Bentham was born into a family of lawyers in Houndsditch, East London on 15 February 1748. He had a prodigious mind. At the age of three, he was found seated at a desk reading Rapin's huge folio *History of England* with a lighted candle on each side of him. At six, he was reading *Telemachus*, the son of Odysseus and Penelope in Homer's *Odyssey*, which he took up as a novel but which he claimed turned him into a philosopher. At the age of seven, he was sent to Westminster School, at 12 to Oxford and at 16 to Lincoln's Inn. He was called to the Bar in 1769 but, being appalled by what he saw as a combination of malpractices and out-dated legal precedents, he quit the profession in order to "put an end to them rather than profit from them".

Lord Brougham wrote of Bentham that,

> The age of Law Reform and the age of Jeremy Bentham are one and the same...No one before him had ever seriously thought of exposing the defects in our English system of Jurisprudence...He it was who made the first mighty step of trying the whole provisions of our jurisprudence by the test of expediency, fearlessly examining how far each part was connected with the rest; and with a yet more undaunted courage, inquiring how far even its most consistent and symmetrical arrangements were framed according to the principle which should pervade a Code of Laws – their adaption to the circumstances of society, to the wants of men, and to the promotion of human happiness.[1]

Bentham stressed that Beccaria had drawn his attention to the principle of the greatest happiness of the greatest number and acknowledged his debt to him on penal law saying that when Beccaria came, he was received as an

---

1. Lord Brougham. (1838) *Speeches*. Edinburgh, Adam and Charles Black. vol. ii. pp. 287-8.

angel from heaven would be by the faithful. He was, he said, the father of the art of legislation.

It is ironic that Bentham declared that the rule of law is a "nonsense on stilts" and that "every law is an infraction of liberty", statements that have led some writers to believe that he disapproved of the rule of law. In fact, however, he was deeply influenced by Beccaria and considered, as part of the rule of law, that people had a right not to have their lives unlawfully taken away and that personal liberty should be protected. He firmly advocated that the law should be written in clear terms in codes that were free from ambiguity, obscurity and bulkiness and made available to all. On torture he agreed in principle with Beccaria but, as we shall see, he considered that in certain rare circumstances it was permissible. What Bentham disliked most were judges and the unwritten common law with its judicial law-making. He set out to replace the common law with a science of law.

In spasms of creative energy Bentham produced codes of law for many countries in the world at large and wrote at length on many topics such as the relationship between law and morals. In all, his published works run to nearly six million words most of which are not relevant here. We should, however, consider some topics as background material for questions relating to his approach to the rule of law.

Law Reform

Despite his scepticism and authoritarian tendencies, Bentham, again following Beccaria, gave birth to Utilitarianism with its principle involving the greatest happiness of the greatest number. It was to be a philosophy of emancipation. In doing so he started a powerful movement for reform and philanthropy and encouraged Romilly, Brougham and others in law reform. His was a seminal influence in a period which saw the birth of capitalism, the emerging working-class and Methodism. He saw the American War of Independence and the French Revolution; the publication of Adam Smith's *Wealth of Nations,* the new ideas of Rousseau, Hume and Paine, the Clapham Sect and – on the day on which he died – the enactment of the Great Reform Act of 1832.

Bentham abhorred the unwritten common law made up of decisions of the judges hallowed by the theory of binding precedent. He claimed that, "Lawyers love unwritten law for the same reason that the Egyptian priest loved hieroglyphics, for the same reason priests of all religions have loved their particular dogmas and mysteries. They are a source of power, reputation and fortune".[2]

The law, therefore, had to be written down, but that was not enough in itself. What was needed was a rational Code, based upon the principle of utility, which would be simple both in its arrangement and in the expression of its contents. This would simplify the machinery of administration whilst at the same time preserving the customary rights of the people in a written and consistent form. Bentham knew there could be no government without law and he sought to rescue law from obscurity and what he saw as a mean and oppressive function.

However, his concept of a completely new code of criminal law replacing the common law was not entirely appealing to the landowners, industrialists and financiers of the early nineteenth century. Furthermore, like a police force a criminal code was not popular with the ordinary people of England who were distrustful of how the police and law codes in France were used in infringing individual liberty. Our common law, and the rule of law, were at least considered to protect the liberty of the subject.

Opposition to the Death Penalty

Bentham was ahead of most of his contemporaries in following Beccaria in being totally opposed to the death penalty. In his *Rationale of Punishment*[3], written in 1775 but published in Paris in 1811 and in London only in 1830, Bentham claimed that the death penalty had the undesirable effect of producing sentiments of pity for the sufferer, with the spectators at the gallows sharing his ordeal. These bloody executions, he said, "... are the real causes

---

2. Jeremy Bentham. (1827) *Rationale of Judicial Evidence, Specially Applied to English Practice.* London, L. Hunt & Clarke. vol. vii.
3. Jeremy Bentham. (1830) *Works.* pp. 1 – 143.

of that deep-rooted antipathy that is felt against the laws and those by whom they are administered; an antipathy which tends to multiply offences by favouring the impunity of the guilty". Such threatened fate also hardened criminals to the feelings of others as well as to their own feelings, and they saw every barbarity they inflicted as a justified reprisal. As, at the time, death by hanging could follow for many trivial offences, such as stealing a handkerchief, or a starving person stealing food worth as little as a shilling, Bentham also saw the fairly frequent resulting leniency of judges and juries as harmful in bringing the law into contempt.

The desirable penal qualities lacking in capital punishment Bentham described as follows:

1. The punishment of death could not be used for compensation as its source was destroyed.
2. Executed men could not be reformed and rendered of some use to society.
3. The death penalty was unequal since men were unequal. Death was the absence of all pleasure but also of all pain, and Bentham believed that many offenders would calculate the balance of each and consider life not worth keeping without the pleasures they could secure only by crime. In such cases punishment of death could be of no use. To this had to be added the criminal's calculation that infliction of the death penalty was by no means certain, and was distant compared with the existing discontent at not possessing the object of his passion.
4. A man might offend by a single and sudden act, oblivious to the prospect of pain to which he was subjecting himself. The death penalty was not variable and the amount of evil could not be increased or reduced.
5. Equally it was not remissible. This was important as judges were not infallible and many innocent victims had perished.

In conclusion, Bentham found the death penalty might be necessary in one case only, and that only occasionally. He agreed with Beccaria that imprisonment might not answer the purpose of safe custody in the case of rebellion, where destroying the chief might be necessary to destroy the faction. In such a case, if discontent were widespread the gaolers could be won over or overpowered. Even with such political offences, however, Bentham had serious doubts and saw that if one dangerous enemy were removed he might be replaced by a more formidable successor.[4]

Radzinowicz states that Bentham thought capital punishment should be imposed for murder only.[5] This is unjust to Bentham, however, since he considered the reasons for complete abolition to be "conclusive". Only if it were retained did he say it should be confined to murder and then only if committed with aggravation.[6] Bentham returned to the subject in 1831 when, at the advanced age of 83, he published in London an essay entitled, *Jeremy Bentham to his Fellow Citizens of France on Death Punishment*. In this he argued for total abolition with no exceptions. The reasons were mainly as before. Inefficiency, irremissibility, a tendency to produce crimes and to enhance the evil effects of undue pardon. He also believed that where it had been abolished crime was reduced.

Torture

On the question of torture Bentham was inconsistent. At first he assumed torture was morally indefensible. But later he came to believe that this was sentimental prejudice and that in some circumstances torture was easier to justify than other punishments.[7] He accepted the justice of Beccaria's observations on torture, but thought there were occasions when it might be used which had no relation to the cases with which Beccaria had been dealing. It is necessary also to understand that Bentham worked from a narrow conception of torture which he defined as making a person suffer violent pain to the body to compel him to do, or desist from, something. Clearly this did not include mental torture. Bentham's purpose was to consider whether torture

---

4. Jeremy Bentham. *Rationale of Punishment. Op. cit.* p. 193.
5. Leon Radzinowicz. (1948) *A History of English Criminal Law and its Administration from 1750. The Movement for Reform.* vol. i. p. 391. Although this position was corrected in volume iv, *Grappling for Control.* p. 326.
6. Jeremy Bentham. *Rationale of Punishment. Op. cit.* p. 196.
7. See Professor Twining. (1973) "Bentham on Torture". *Northern Ireland Legal Quarterly.* No. 3. vol. xxiv. p. 305.

might usefully be used in place of other punishments which he believed caused greater hardship.

To Bentham what distinguished torture from other punishments was that the attainment of its purpose was plainly seen and it could instantly be stopped. Hence, he concluded that there were two cases in which torture might properly be used:

1. Where the thing a man was required to do was something in his power to do and which the public had an interest in his doing. In this case so long as he continued to suffer for not doing it he was sure not to be innocent. Examples given by Bentham of crimes where this might be applicable were incendiarism, aggravated murder, and assassination for hire.
2. Where it was only probably in his power to do something and where, for not doing it, he might suffer although innocent, but where the public interest was so great that an innocent person's suffering was the lesser evil. This could only arise where the safety of the whole state was endangered.

Professor Twining gives the following modern-day example as explaining Bentham's position: "It is believed that an atomic bomb has been placed somewhere in a major city with a timing device attached to it. X, who is believed to have information about the location of this bomb, has been captured".[8] Similar reasoning to the second conclusion has now been used, in recent times, in regard to detainees in Guantánamo Bay and to extraordinary rendition.

The difficulty is that Bentham was prepared to institutionalise torture without paying sufficient regard to the difficulty of preventing its abuse and its breach of the principle of the presumption of innocence. Not all Utilitarians were prepared to support his acceptance of torture and many preferred Beccaria's appeal to principles of justice and humanity. Clearly torture is in breach of the concept of the rule of law.

---

8. *Ibid.* p. 346.

Jeremy Bentham

Analysis of Punishment

In his *Rationale of Punishment,* Bentham argued that all punishment was itself an evil. It was a kind of "counter-crime" committed with the authority of the law. But, upon the principle of utility it was to be permitted in so far as it promised to exclude some greater evil. In fact, in this book Bentham analysed the whole subject of punishment in a scientific manner for the first time in history. Romilly said of it that, "penal legislation hitherto has resembled what the science of physic must have been when physicians did not know the properties and effects of the medicines they administered".

To Bentham, as with Beccaria, the vital object of punishment was to protect society and not to inflict torments on the offender. He was totally opposed to transportation which he considered was unequal in its effect on different individuals. It also had little deterrent value by example to others and was wasteful of both lives and money. After rotting in the hulks for a year or two, he declared, a miserable wretch was crammed with hundreds of other into a floating prison in which he faced the risks of famine, disease and death, only to reach a life of slavery, suffering and misery. In its place he wanted to see three different kinds of imprisonment adapted for prisoners who had committed offences of differing degrees of seriousness.

Bentham was a brilliant progeny of the Enlightenment but his work suffered from serious defects. The pursuit of happiness, which meant abundance, equality and security, predominated in his plans over the pursuit of justice and prevention of cruelty. His elimination of motive took all meaning out of morality. And, he failed to see criminals as complicated human beings. Moreover, he had no perception of the achievements of Garrow and the advent of adversary trial and rules of criminal evidence. Nevertheless, his influence on law reform was far-reaching throughout the nineteenth century and beyond and he inspired the more practical minds of Romilly, Peel, Brougham and the Criminal Law Commissioners to effect the bringing of our criminal law out of its dark, medieval past into the modern world.

Indeed, speaking of Bentham's treatise on punishments, Romilly said that it appeared to have extraordinary merit, and to be likely to be more popular than most of Bentham's writings and to produce very good effects. "Since the work of Beccaria", he continued, "nothing has appeared on the subject of Criminal Law which has made any impression on the public. This work will, I think, probably make a very deep impression".[9]

Despite his own protestations (perhaps tongue in cheek) to the contrary, it seems clear that Bentham's philosophy and his works encompassed many of the principles of the rule of law. He opposed the harshness of the criminal law and judicial law-making as well as the death penalty and, in the main, state torture. He wanted to demystify the criminal law and make it more civilized and less arbitrary than it had been which must be a consequence of adopting the rule of law.

Death

Bentham had the rather macabre idea that on his death his body should be preserved and kept on display. He died on 6 June 1832 and his body was indeed preserved and is kept at University College London in a wooden cabinet. Fortunately, his ideas are more widely available in bookshops and on the internet. Unfortunately, the pursuit of happiness meant more to him than the pursuit of justice and the prevention of cruelty. Nevertheless, his influence on law reform was far-reaching throughout the nineteenth century and he remains a serious intellectual force for any critique of the English legal system.

Moreover, apart from Bentham's agreement with Beccaria on many aspects of penal reform, they also shared views on the nature of the rule of law. Both contrasted the spirit of tyranny with clear comprehensive legislative enactments. They disliked judicial law-making and discretion, *ex post facto* legislation and they believed men should be presented with the law clearly as also with the consequences of disobedience.[10] Despite Bentham's prolific work and influence on penal law he fully acknowledged a tremendous debt to Beccaria.

---

9. Sir Samuel Romilly. (1840) *The Memoirs of Sir Samuel Romilly Written by Himself and Edited by his Sons.* London, John Murray, vol. ii, pp. 259.
10. H.L.A. Hart. (1982) *Essays on Bentham: Jurisprudence and Political Theory.* Oxford, Clarendon Press. pp. 47-8.

CHAPTER 8

THOMAS ERSKINE

England's foremost advocate

Garrow made his name, and established prisoners' rights in the criminal law, in the sordid surroundings of the eighteenth century Old Bailey. Erskine, on the other hand, shone in the state trials that rocked England and Scotland when, in 1794, the government of William Pitt took fright at the turn of events in the French Revolution which threatened Great Britain with its own reign of terror. He had a passion for liberty that he was able to pass on to juries and made a lasting contribution to it. In a sense he was able to help make history.

Erskine was one of the foremost forensic advocates ever to appear in English criminal courts and his greatest claim to fame came with his defence, without fee, of the prisoners in the great treason trials held in London in 1794; trials that threatened to destroy the rule of law. *Habeas corpus* had been suspended, the Old Bailey was surrounded by troops, and a Special Powers Act was threatened, all to deal with an imagined revolutionary insurrection. No less than 800 warrants were prepared to arrest people who were merely calling for franchise reform but were to be charged with "compassing the death of the King" in what historians call "The English Terror". There was an open presumption of guilt and no question of proof beyond reasonable doubt. As if to make the situation clear, with their lives at risk Edmund Burke accused them of being assassins and he urged that the disease of the body politic demanded the "critical terrors of the cautery and the knife".

The court sat with a special commission of six judges, presided over by Lord Chief Justice Eyre. With indignation Erskine not only set out to prove his clients innocent but he also undertook to finish the task he had started earlier in his defence of Lord George Gordon – to cut down the law of constructive treason. Treason, he reminded the jury, was to plot against the King's life, not merely to offend his government. As Attorney-General, Sir

John Scott, later Lord Chancellor Eldon, led the prosecuting team which included William Garrow. In unprecedented scenes Erskine wooed the jury in a speech that lasted over seven hours to such effect that he decisively turned the first three trials against the government. And his triumph was transparent when each of the prisoners was found not guilty. Erskine was fêted by the huge crowds massed outside the court in every direction. The remaining warrants were consigned to the rubbish bin and England's freedom was secure.[1]

Garrow and Erskine were contemporaries and friends who sometimes appeared in court in the same trials either in harness or as opponents. Both rose from rags to riches, earned huge fees and, more importantly, by sheer skill and eloquence they came to be regarded as two of the brightest stars ever to shine in English criminal courts. Both proved able to empathise with juries and somehow infuse their ideas into the minds of those twelve good men and true before whom they so frequently appeared. In the courtroom Erskine stood thin and erect and had a clear and melodic voice and a penetrating eye. But Garrow's questioning of hostile witnesses was more inventive. Whilst Garrow unwittingly revolutionised the face of English criminal law, and thereby the rule of law, Erskine was perhaps the most eloquent open advocate and champion of justice and the rule of law in English legal history.

Family background

Erskine, who was born in Edinburgh on 10 January 1750, came from a family of great repute in Scotland. Thomas, the first Lord Erskine, married the granddaughter of James I of Scotland and the family was close to Mary Queen of Scots. Through the centuries they had a long connection with the aristocracy and royalty of Scotland as the Earls of Buchan until Erskine's father, the 10th earl, found himself in straightened circumstances. As a result he was forced to move the family home from the ancestral castle. First to small, ill-furnished upper rooms in the Old Town of Edinburgh and later

---

1. For more about Thomas Erskine see John Hostettler (2010) *Thomas Erskine and Trial by Jury*. Hook, Hampshire, Waterside Press.

to St. Andrews, Fife where they could live even more cheaply than in the Old Town. The mother of young Thomas was Agnes Steuart, the daughter of Sir James Steuart, Solicitor-General of Scotland. She possessed a powerful and cultivated intellect and undertook the early stages of his education.

Public school and university were financially out of the question although for a few months Thomas managed to attend some classes at Edinburgh University. But he did move among circles which included peers, lawyers and government ministers and this provided an invaluable education in itself and gave him the confidence and a familiarity with persons of influence which were both to serve him so well. On leaving St Andrews Grammar School in Fife he desired to enter a profession but his parents could not afford the expense involved. In consequence, at the age of 14 he went to sea as a midshipman. Once in the royal navy, he wore the traditional blue jacket, cocked hat and sword and served for four years in the *Tartar,* a man-of-war commanded by the experienced sea captain, Sir David Lindsay.

Youth

When Erskine was 18 years of age his father died at Bath and was succeeded as Earl by his eldest son, David Steuart. Although receiving no inheritance from his father, by this time Thomas could afford to leave the navy, where he had become acting lieutenant, and join the army as an ensign in the Royals, or 1st Regiment of Foot. It is significant that when in the army he spent two years in Minorca where he found time to study English literature and learn many of Shakespeare's famous speeches by heart. And, when on leave in London he joined the social and intellectual life of the capital and was on friendly terms with Dr Johnson, Edmund Burke and Edward Gibbon. It was whilst in the army that he fell in love with Frances Moore, the daughter of Daniel Moore, the Member of Parliament for Marlow. On 21 April 1770 they married in spite some opposition from his family. However, it was to prove a lasting and happy marriage. It was also whilst in the army that he wrote a bold and eloquent pamphlet entitled, *Observations on the Prevailing Abuses in the British Army, arising from the Corruption of Civil Government.* To this he added the sub-title, *A Proposal to the Officers towards obtaining an Addition to their pay.* Despite this sweetener, and an assurance to fellow officers that they would not be punished for mutiny, he published the pamphlet anonymously. Nevertheless, his authorship was an open secret and the pamphlet was widely circulated.

Erskine's purpose was to rouse officers to demand that soldiers be able to enjoy all the rights of citizens. In his arguments we can discern the genesis of the advocate of the future. And he was to be encouraged by the knowledge that when the American War of Independence revealed deficiencies in the British army it adopted and benefitted considerably from some of the reforms he had proposed.

Freedom of the Press

One day, purely by chance and wearing his army uniform, Erskine wandered into an Assizes court presided over by Lord Mansfield. Listening to the trial he became so confident that he could do better than the eloquent leaders of the circuit before him that he resolved to study law and become a barrister. He sold his army commission to provide some finance and joined Lincoln's Inn on 26 April 1775, paying an enrolment fee of £3.3.4d. Three years later he was called to the Bar.

In all of Erskine's early cases, with his speeches to juries he can be seen resolutely upholding the rule of law. His eloquence was such that his reputation was assured from the start. But he defended freedom at every available opportunity and did much to destroy the iniquitous law of constructive treason. In 1783 he received a silk gown to become King's Counsel and was appointed Attorney-General to the Prince of Wales.

Despite his friendship with the Prince of Wales, Erskine continued to defend men accused of sedition and treason and in the case of the *House of Commons v. Stockdale* he made what Lord John Campbell described as "the finest speech ever delivered at the English Bar; [a speech] that won a verdict which forever established the freedom of the press in England".[2] The trial involved the prosecution, by the House of Commons in the name of the

---

2. Lord John Campbell. (1847) *Lives of the Chancellors.* London, John Murray. vol. vi. p. 443.

Attorney-General, of John Stockdale, a respectable bookseller in Piccadilly. The charge was for an alleged libel upon the Commons in a book about the impeachment of Warren Hastings in the House of Lords which Stockdale published in the regular course of his business. In it the House was compared with an Inquisition in its impeachment of Hastings for alleged high crimes and misdemeanours in Bengal. The trial came before Lord Kenyon and a Special Jury on 9 December 1789.[3] Special Juries were composed of twelve "well-born and educated men" drawn from a special panel of men with a much higher property qualification than was the case with the normal petty jury of "twelve good men and true".

In opening the prosecution case, the Attorney-General, Sir Archibald Macdonald, deplored what he called the licentiousness of the press and proceeded to inform the jury that, "the liberty of the press consists in its good regulation ... it must be from time to time lopped of its unjust excesses". In contrast, Erskine, whose defence was that the alleged libel was a *bonâ fide* defence of Warren Hastings, put a stark proposition to the jury. He told them that if they thought the book to be the work of a man with an intelligent mind and compassion for a fellow man he believed to be innocent but nevertheless convicted him, they would not only cause an injustice but would break up the press of England and surrender its rights and liberties for ever.

After painting a colourful picture of the impeachment which was proceeding in the House of Lords, Erskine said that it could not be endured that Hastings should suffer without being permitted to have something submitted to the judgment of mankind in his defence. If that were the law (which, he claimed, it was for the jury to decide) then he would have no trial. Instead, "that great hall, built by our fathers for English justice, is no longer a court, but an altar; and an Englishman, instead of being judged in it by *God and his Country* is a *Victim and a Sacrifice*".

---

3. William Cobbett's *State Trials*.(1789) vol. xxii. col. 237.

The Indian Chief

Erskine then addressed the jury in what Lord John Campbell went on to describe as "the finest passage to be found in ancient or modern oratory – for imagery, for passion, for pathos, for variety and beauty of cadence, for the concealment of art, for effect in gaining the object of the orator".[4] Even if there is perhaps some hyperbole here it will give some impression of Erskine's style and power to reproduce some of the speech in detail although it better suited the age in which he made it than would be the case today.

> It may, and must be true, Erskine said, that Mr Hastings has repeatedly offended against the rights and privileges of Asiatic government, if he was the faithful deputy of a power which could not maintain itself for an hour without trampling upon both; he may and must have offended against the laws of God and nature, if he was the faithful viceroy of an empire wrested in blood from the people to whom God and nature had given it; he may and must have preserved that unjust dominion over timorous and abject nations by a terrifying, overbearing, insulting superiority, if he was the faithful administrator of your government, which having no root in consent or affection, no foundation in similarities of interests, nor support from any one principle which cements men together in society, could only be upheld by alternate stratagem and force.

> The unhappy people of India, feeble and effeminate as they are from the softness of their climate, and subdued and broken as they have been by the knavery and strength of civilization, still occasionally start up in all the vigour and intelligence of insulted nature; to be governed at all, they must be governed with a rod of iron; and our empire in the East would, long since, have been lost to Great Britain, if civil skill and military prowess had not united their efforts to support an authority – which Heaven never gave, by means which it can never sanction.

> Gentlemen, I think I can observe that you are touched with this way of considering the subject; and I can account for it. I have not been considering it through the cold medium of books, but have been speaking of man and his nature, and of human dominion, from what I have seen of them myself amongst reluctant nations submitting to our authority. I know what they feel, and how such feelings can alone be repressed. I have heard them in my youth from a naked savage, in the indignant character of a prince surrounded by his subjects, addressing the Governor of a

---

4. Lord John Campbell. *Lives of the Chancellors. Op. cit.* p. 447.

British colony, holding a bundle of sticks in his hand, as the notes of his unlettered eloquence: "Who is it"? said the jealous ruler over the desert, encroached upon by the restless foot of English adventure – "who is it that causes this river to rise in the high mountains, and to empty itself into the ocean? Who is it that causes to blow the loud winds of winter, and that calms them again in the summer? Who is it that rears up the shade of those lofty forests, and blasts them with the quick lightening at his pleasure? The same Being who gave to you a country on the other side of the waters, and gave ours to us; and by this title we will defend it", said the warrior, throwing down his tomahawk upon the ground, and raising the war-sound of his nation.

These are the feelings of subjugated man all round the globe; and depend upon it, nothing but fear will control where it is vain to look for affection...it might be better perhaps to think of perpetually securing [justice] by recalling our troops and our merchants, and abandoning our oriental empire. Until this be done, neither religion nor philosophy can be pressed very far into the aid of reformation and punishment. If England, from a lust of ambition and domination, will insist on maintaining despotic rule over distant and hostile nations, and gives commission to her viceroys to govern them with no other instructions than to preserve them, and to secure permanently their revenues; with what colour of consistency or reason can she place herself in the moral chair, and affect to be shocked at the execution of her own orders; adverting to the exact measure of wickedness and injustice necessary to their execution, and complaining only of the *excess* as the immorality, considering her authority as a dispensation for breaking the commands of God, and the breach of them as only punishable when contrary to the ordinances of man.

Reverting to the book, Erskine continued that he was against punishing strong opinions which might be expressed with no evil intent when a writer warmed to his subject. Otherwise minds would be silenced by the terrors of punishment and this would deny the people works of genius that could expand the boundaries of human reason.

Under such terrors, he said, all the great lights of science and civilisation would be extinguished. Men would be unable to communicate their free thoughts to one another if a lash were held over them. It was the nature of all things that were great and useful to be wild and irregular. We had to accept them with their alloys, or live without them. "Tempests occasionally shake our dwellings and dissipate our commerce, but they scourge before them the lazy elements which without them would stagnate into pestilence".

In the same way, he continued, liberty had to be taken as it was. It might be reduced to regularity and be shaped into a perfect model of severe law. But it would then not be liberty and we would die under the "lash of such unyielding injustice" which had been taken in exchange for freedom.

Towards the end of his speech to the jury Erskine expressed the hope that he had performed his duty to his client. He had been urged on, he declared, by his love of justice, and the country's constitution which was the inheritance of the world. These were the motives which had animated him in defence of a person who was a stranger to him and whose shop he had never entered. They might not be relevant in cases involving property or unjust libels. But in this case they were when the issue involved was not a question of law but a pure question of fact.

The speech apparently had the desired effect and, although the jury was a Special Jury, after retiring for two hours it returned a unanimous verdict of not guilty.

Spellbinding Eloquence

After Erskine had concluded his speech the Attorney-General, in amazed admiration, declared that, "My learned friend and I stand very much contrasted with each other in this case. To him belong infinite eloquence and ingenuity, a gift of persuasion beyond that which I almost ever knew fall to any man's share, and a power of language greater than that which ever met my ear".

Lord Chief Baron Abinger, who was in court, described to Lord Campbell the effect of the speech on those present. "They all actually believed", he said, "that they saw before them the Indian chief with his bundle of sticks and his tomahawk. Their breasts thrilled with the notes of his unlettered eloquence and they thought they heard him raise the war-sound of his nation".[5]

Lord Brougham later wrote that there were no finer things in modern, and few finer in ancient, eloquence than the celebrated passage of the Indian chief. Nor had beautiful language ever been used with more curious felicity

---

5. *Ibid.* p. 450.

to raise a striking and appropriate image before the mind than in the simile of the winds "lashing before them the lazy elements, without which the tempest would stagnate into pestilence".[6]

Such impressions cannot be absorbed simply by reading the speech. We cannot hear or see what the *Edinburgh Review* described as, "the witchery of this extraordinary man's voice, eye and action".[7] And Brougham went on to describe Erskine's voice as of surpassing sweetness, clear, flexible, strong, earnest and free from harshness or monotony. Juries had declared, he said, that they felt it impossible to remove their eyes from him when he had riveted and fascinated them by his first glance. He had a thorough knowledge of men, their passions and feelings. He was lively and brilliant. "He knew every avenue to the heart, and could at will make all its chords vibrate to his touch".[8]

In an age when democracy was widely derided, and exploitation was regarded as desirable when exercised in the cause of commerce, Erskine in his speech exposed the raw nerve of colonial rule. In excusing Hastings personally from the charge of corruption (and he was eventually found not guilty on his impeachment), he nevertheless revealed the inhumanity involved for millions of people in the strategy which Hastings was charged to put into effect. In doing so he exhibited a sensibility, that was not always perceived by his contemporary admirers, towards human beings who were subjected to indignity, loss of freedom and often death far away by policy dictated from Westminster. As he told the jury, Erskine was animated by his love of justice and this encompassed liberty and the rule of law.

John Frost

In 1793 Erskine defended John Frost, an attorney, before a Special Jury on a charge of speaking seditious words at the Percy coffee house in London.[9]

---

6. Henry Brougham. (1839) *Historical Sketches of Statesmen who Flourished in the Time of George III*. London, Charles Knight & Co. p. 242.
7. *Edinburgh Review*. (1810)
8. Henry Brougham. *Historical Sketches. Op. cit.* pp. 237-8.
9. Howell's *State Trials. Op. cit.* col. 472.

The words were spoken after a dinner and a good deal of drink, and following provocation. In any event, all that he had said was that he was for equality and no King and in favour of improving the franchise. Even the Attorney-General, in prosecuting, conceded that to espouse the doctrine of "Equality and no King" had long been held not to infringe the right of free speech. But times had changed, he argued, and with the French Revolution across the Channel, punishment was now justified.

In response, Erskine asked the jury:

> Must an English gentleman in future fill his wine by a measure, lest in the openness of his soul, and whilst believing his neighbours are joining with him in that happy relaxation and freedom of thought which is the prime blessing of life, he should find his character blasted, and his person in a prison? Does any man put such constraint upon himself in the most private moment of his life, that he would be contented to have his loosest and lightest words recorded, and set in array against him in a court of justice? Thank God, the world lives very differently, or it would not be worth living in.

After more words in a similar vein, he continued:

> When I came down this morning, and found contrary to my expectation, that we were to be stuffed into this miserable hole in the wall [the Court of Common Pleas] to consume our constitutions, suppose I had muttered along through the gloomy passages...Are we to have no respite? Are we to die of asthma in this damned corner? I wish to God the roof would come down...such words would be irreverent and foolish.

But, he added, if such expressions had been imputed to him by a malignant mind, how would they have been treated in the House of Commons on a motion for his expulsion? The witness would have been laughed out of the House as a great blockhead before he had half finished.

The witnesses against Frost, who had initiated the prosecution, were described by Erskine as the government's well-paid spies and informers. Society was under the lash of such "wretched vermin" bent on hunting men in the privacy of their domestic lives. Such a vexatious system of inquisition began and ended with the Star Chamber; the common law of England never knew it. "Her noble, dignified and humane policy soars above the little irregularities of our lives, and disdains to enter our closets without a warrant". Otherwise, where then was the presumption of innocence.

Notwithstanding Erskine's eloquence, atrocities were taking place in France and the Special Jury found Frost guilty. However, Erskine won the cheers of the crowds outside the court and eventually, in 1813, Frost received a royal pardon.

Trial of Tom Paine

During this period Erskine was engaged in many high profile civil cases that secured him a considerable income. Indeed he was probably the highest paid member of the Bar of all time in real terms, although on occasion, as in the treason trials of 1794, he acted without fee. At the same time he continued to appear for the defence in state trials that threatened liberty including the defence of Tom Paine on a charge of seditious libel. Under attack were Paine's projects of social reform in Part 2 of his book *The Rights of Man* which sold over a million and a half copies – a colossal figure for the time. It is noteworthy that no prosecution had followed the earlier publication of Part 1 of the book which sold fewer copies. The charge was meant to be preliminary to a prosecution for high treason and on the advice of the poet William Blake, Paine fled to Paris where he had been elected to the National Convention. The trial was held *in absentia* before Lord Chief Justice Kenyon and a Special Jury on 18 December 1792.[10]

Erskine was told by Lord Loughborough to decline the brief for Paine but, independent and fearless as ever, he vigorously declined to do so. As a consequence he was dismissed from his position as legal adviser to the Prince of Wales. He did, however, establish the "cab-rank" rule (considered at the present time to be the "glory of the Bar") whereby a barrister must accept any brief to appear in a court in which he practises. In fact, the rule is now enshrined in paragraph 602 of the *Code of Conduct of the English Bar.* In a brilliant exposition of the principles involved, Erskine said,

---

10. Howell's *State Trials. Op. cit.* col. 358.

I will forever, at all hazards, assert the dignity, independence and integrity of the English Bar, without which impartial justice, the most valuable part of the English Constitution, can have no existence. From the moment that any advocate can be permitted to say that he will, or will not, stand between the Crown and the subject arraigned in the court where he daily sits to practise, from that moment the liberties of England are at an end. If the advocate refuses to defend, from what he may think of the charge or of the defence, he assumes the character of the Judge; nay, he assumes it before the hour of judgment; and, in proportion to his rank and reputation, puts the heavy influence of, perhaps, a mistaken opinion into the scale against the accused, in whose favour the benevolent principle of English law makes all presumptions.

Despite the subsequent acceptance of his stand, at the time there was considerable clamour against him in society for taking on the case.

In his defence of Paine, Erskine examined the history of freedom of thought and the rule of law in England and declared that although Paine's opinions did not conform with government policy, "I maintain", he stressed, that *opinion* is free and that *conduct* alone is amenable to the law". Again, an unwritten aspect of the rule of law. In this case, however, the Special Jury fulfilled its appointed role and found Paine guilty before the Attorney-General had replied to Erskine or the Judge had had an opportunity to sum up the case. Paine was sentenced to the medieval punishment of outlawry by which his property was forfeit and he was to be executed if he returned to England.

Treason Trials

It was now that Erskine reached the height of his career and his efforts for liberty and the rule of law in the infamous treason trials of 1794 mentioned at the opening of this chapter. These three trials formed a watershed in English history and without Erskine's part in them our lives would be very different today. The background to the trials was the French Revolution and the ferocious bloodletting of its Reign of Terror.

At this time in England there was a considerable movement for reform of the franchise. Corruption in electoral contests was widespread. Large cities like Manchester had no MPs whilst Old Sarum with no population sent two Members to the House of Commons. Even William Pitt, on 7 May

1782, had introduced a motion in the Commons calling for a select committee to consider parliamentary reform. It was defeated but, undaunted, Pitt later introduced three resolutions to prevent bribery in elections and attack corrupt boroughs. These too failed. Progress was slow and, with economic distress widespread in England, the early promise of the French Revolution brought into being a number of societies which entered into correspondence with French political clubs. When France declared war on Britain in 1793 they were quickly branded as seditious.

This enabled Pitt's government to turn its back on electoral reform and in a panic based upon an unjustified fear of the French Revolution spreading to England they suspended *habeas corpus*, and announced the discovery of a huge revolutionary plot. At the same time they arrested Thomas Hardy, a shoemaker, John Horne Tooke, an elderly clergyman and philologist, and John Thelwall, a Jacobite, all active in corresponding societies. According to Macaulay:

> In Pitt's domestic policy there was at this time assuredly no want of vigour. While he offered to French Jacobins a resistance so feeble that it only encouraged the evil which he wished to suppress, he put down English Jacobinism with a strong hand...It was hardly safe for a republican to avow his political creed over his beefsteak and his bottle of port at a chophouse...He [Pitt] was all feebleness and languor in his conflict with the foreign enemy who was really to be dreaded, and reserved all his energy and resolution for the domestic enemy who might safely have been despised.[11]

And, Winston Churchill, writing about this moment in history, said, "In England the Government had been forced to take repressive measures of a sternness unknown for generations. Republican lecturers were swept into prison. The Habeas Corpus Act was suspended. Distinguished writers were put on their trial for treason; *but juries could not be prevailed to convict*".[12] They had done so, however, on similar trials in Scotland, which had a legal system based on Roman-canon law and where juries were hand-picked by

---

11. Thomas Babington Macaulay. (1980) *A History of England in the Eighteenth Century*. London, Folio Society edition. pp. 198-9.
12. Italics added by the author of this work. Winston Churchill. (1957) *A History of the English-Speaking Peoples*. London, Cassell & Co., vol. iii. p. 249.

the judges. Moreover, in Scotland the judges were more partisan than in England and there was no Erskine for the defence. At the time, in both England and Scotland, the land swarmed with spies and informers willing, in return for payment, to give evidence against reformers. As part of the psychological warfare against the English prisoners (who were held in the Tower of London) Pitt took to the House of Commons three huge sealed bags of captured documents and a message from the King requiring the enactment of a Special Powers Act. Yet the accused had merely called a Convention to seek means of securing reform in the representation of the people in Parliament. Notwithstanding their acknowledged moderation they were charged with high treason although it was never suggested that they threatened the life of the King or advocated any violence whatsoever.

Thomas Hardy was put on trial first. At no time in the past had a treason trial lasted for more than a day. This one was to continue for eight days with the court sitting from eight in the morning to the early hours after midnight. Erskine himself addressed the jury for seven hours. Referring to the alleged possibility of meetings leading to disorder he took his usual position and said, "I protest in his [Hardy's] name against all speculations respecting *consequences* when the law commands us to look only to *intentions*". He also aggressively cross-examined prosecution witnesses in the style of William Garrow who, interestingly, in this trial appeared as one of the prosecuting counsel for the Crown.

By the end of his final speech to the jury, which lasted from two o'clock in the afternoon until nine in the evening, Erskine was so exhausted and hoarse that he could only whisper his peroration and express confidence that the jury would ensure that justice prevailed. Despite his affliction, his quietly-spoken words swept around the still courtroom and, when he finished, there was uproar in his favour which spread to the people still crowding the streets around the court. The verdict of the jury was not guilty.

The trials of John Horne Tooke and John Thelwall, with Erskine again defending, took a similar course and ended with the same result. This led Brougham to say, "Before such a precious service as this may the lustre of statesmen and orators grow pale".[13]

---

13. Henry, Lord Brougham. *Historical Sketches*. *Op cit.*

On 5 January 1795, in the House of Commons, Erskine spoke in support of a motion by Richard Brinsley Sheridan to repeal the Habeas Corpus Suspension Act.[14] In the course of the debate, he received an unusually friendly reception when he said the juries in the treason trials had revealed the falsehood and absurdity of the alleged sedition and conspiracy. He asked, who would defend the country if the threat of invasion from France came about? Only the people could do it and they would do so only if they felt they were defending liberty.

In the parliamentary session of 1795-6 he also strenuously opposed the Seditious Meetings Bill which made most public meetings illegal. He believed the Bills threatened the liberty of the subject, and said he should never cease to struggle in support of liberty. Had not Pitt the Elder, he demanded, said it was the right of a people to resist a government which exercised tyranny and that they should defend their freedom by the last extremity to which free men could resort?

Lord Chancellor

When the Whigs eventually came to power in 1806 with the Ministry of All the Talents, Erskine was appointed as Lord Chancellor. He was not the first choice, however, and the appointment led to some public dissatisfaction since he knew little of the specialised subject of equity. As Romilly wrote in his memoirs, "... he is totally unfit for the situation. His practice has never led him into the courts of equity; and the doctrines which prevail in them are to him almost like the law of a foreign country".[15] Indeed, the Great Seal had already been offered to Lord Mansfield who declined it because of his age and Lord Ellenborough who did so because he was unacquainted with the courts of equity.

Romilly was proved correct. Erskine failed to shine as Chancellor and, with the fall of the government the following year, his tenure came to an

---

14. *Parliamentary History.* (1795) vol. xxxi, p. 1087.
15. Samuel Romilly. (1840) *Memoirs of the Life of Sir Samuel Romilly Written by Himself and Edited by his Sons.* London, John Murray, vol. ii, p. 134.

abrupt end. Unfortunately he was not permitted to return to the Bar and he came to regret ever accepting the Great Seal which he had to give up so soon. And, his disappointment at having to leave the Woolsack was plain when a navigator, upon being asked at a party, on what he had lived when frozen up at the North Pole, replied that he and his companions had lived upon seals. "And a very good living too", interrupted Erskine, "if you keep them long enough". At another party, held on a lawn, he approached a monkey which had a long white hairy mantle flowing gracefully over his head and shoulders and to the amusement of bystanders said, "Sir, I sincerely wish you joy – you wear your wig for life"[16]. Finally, after a last intervention against the prosecution in the House of Lords of Queen Caroline for alleged adultery, he died of pneumonia on 17 November 1823 at the age of 73. At the height of his fame members of the public bought thousands of portraits and busts of him and a hundred cities offered him their freedom.

Sequel

The mid-nineteenth century Middle Temple lawyer, Archer Polson, described Erskine as an intrepid advocate who, with great nerve and courage, acted in the best interests of his clients. He was, he wrote, able to portray forcible images from his vivid imagination in language of transparent beauty.[17] But he added that, Erskine "would often take laudanum to assist him in speaking. It excited his imagination and enabled him to make those brilliant appeals to the jury in which he manifested his great powers. Much of the eloquence he owed to his high animal spirits, without such let no one hope to be a *great* orator!"[18]

Of course, many drugs which are illegal today were not so in Erskine's time and it may be that if they were commonly taken they would arouse no comment. However, I have not been able to trace any corroboration of this suggestion by any other source.

---

16. Lord John Campbell. *Lives of the Chancellors. Op. cit.* vol. vi. p. 621.
17. Archer Polson. (1841) *Law and Lawyers, or Sketches and Illustrations of Legal History and Biography*. Philadelphia, Carey & Hart. vol. i.
18. *Ibid.* p. 201.

As we have seen, in 1806 Erskine was appointed Lord Chancellor and later he became a vain old man. But that is life. What we remember is that his success in upholding liberty and the rule of law in a time of dangerous, heavy-handed repression secured the future for the English people. His career in the law was an example to all future generations of barristers. But, more than that, we are all forever deeply in his debt and his fame is imperishable.

Champions of the Rule of Law

CHAPTER 9

SIR SAMUEL ROMILLY

Self-effacing

Samuel Romilly came to fame as an outstanding criminal law reformer with a firm belief in the rule of law. Nevertheless, he suffered from a self-effacing nature. Macaulay said of him that the only blemish on his spotless character was that he despised popularity too much and too visibly. However, at the same time, he significantly added, his modesty was linked with a remarkable self-possession. Although elected to the House of Commons Romilly never solicited a single constituency vote and never showed himself to the electors until he had been returned at the head of the poll. Shunning publicity he laboured in the shadows. At the same time the cause of penal reform advanced slowly despite all his valiant efforts.[1] Brougham, for his part, believed him to be, "a person of the most natural and simple manners, and one in whom the kindest charities and warmest feelings of human nature were blended in the largest measure with firmness of purpose and unrelaxed sincerity of principle".[2]

However, despite the obvious truth of these assessments they ignore both the entrenched opposition Romilly always encountered to his humanitarian crusade as well as the powerful stimulus he gave to his successors in the struggle for criminal law reform that eventually led to substantial success. He was an Enlightenment figure among others of his time including Jeremy Bentham and Henry Brougham. He was influenced by their writings and also particularly by Beccaria's prodigious and largely utilitarian treatise about which he wrote to his friend and future brother-in-law, the Rev, John Roget,

---

1. Thomas Babington Macaulay. (1980) *A History of England in the Eighteenth Century*. London, Folio Society edition. p. 250.
2. Henry, Lord Brougham. (1839) *Historical Sketches of Statesmen who Flourished in the Time of George III*.

that, "I have lately read a second time, Beccaria on *Crimes and Punishments*, a favourite book, I know, of yours, and I think deservedly".[3]

Background

Samuel Romilly was born at 18 Frith Street in London's Soho on 1 March 1757.[4] His father, Peter Romilly, was a watchmaker and jeweller in that cosmopolitan district of London after his own father had arrived there as a Huguenot refugee from the religious tyranny of Louis XIV. The young Samuel was to attend a local school where he was later to recall that his master had been ignorant, severe and brutal. But even at this early age, Romilly perceived that increasing severity of punishment on boys produced not conformity but lawlessness in proportion to the severity with which they were treated. It was a lesson that was to remain in the forefront of his mind when he later encountered the demand for increased severity in the already insensitive and bloody criminal law.

As he grew older he studied law, history and the classics before working for a time in his father's shop. By his own account he had gone three times through the whole of Livy, Sallust, and Tacitus. He had read all Cicero and the most celebrated of his orations as well as Virgil, Horace, Ovid and Juvenal. Many of these works he translated in verse. To improve his style he also read and studied Addison, Swift, Robertson and Hume.

He left his father's employment to become articled to a solicitor but, like Garrow before him, he decided that he would prefer the life of a barrister and on 3 May 1778, aged 21, he entered Gray's Inn for what he called his, "painful study of the law". When Gray's Inn, in which many Roman Catholics resided, was attacked in the anti-Catholic frenzy of the Gordon Riots in 1780, Romilly spent several nights armed and standing as sentry at its narrow Holborn gate defending the Inn from attack. Fortunately he was

---

3. Extract from a letter dated 1 March 1782. Cited by Leon Radzinowicz. (1948) *A History of English Criminal Law and its Administration from 1750*. Vol. i. *The Movement for Reform.* London, Stevens & Sons Limited. p. 315.
4. Some of what appears in this chapter is taken from Romilly's own *Memoirs of the Life of Sir Samuel Romilly Written by Himself and Edited by his Sons*. (1840) 3 vols. London, John Murray.

not injured or killed. Subsequently, after being called to the Bar on the last day of the Easter term of 1783 he started to practise on the Midland Circuit and then spent the rest of his life endeavouring to ameliorate the cruel and archaic penal system which besmirched England's name.

At that time, what is known as the "Bloody Code" contained well over 200 crimes which, if proved, generally led to the gallows. Romilly was to refer to it as, "Our sanguinary and barbarous penal code, written in blood". Virtually all felonies were punishable with death, although sentences could be mitigated by royal pardon or "pious perjury" whereby juries often reduced the value of stolen goods so that an offence ceased to be capital. The alternative to the gallows was then transportation to Botany Bay for, seven, fourteen or twenty-one years.

Not only men but women and children too could be sentenced to death for trivial offences. Take the case of Nicholas White in 1833. Only nine years of age he was playing a game of "dare" in the street with a number of other children. He was tempted, as part of the game, to push a stick through a cracked window and pull out some printers' colours. Despite their value being only twopence he was tried at the Old Bailey for housebreaking convicted and sentenced to be hanged by the neck until dead under a statute Romilly had endeavoured unsuccessfully to have repealed. I have been unable to trace whether he was actually executed or transported. Either way, the case is a terrible indictment of the criminal law that so appalled Romilly.

Death Penalty

In a letter dated 9 May 1783 to the Reverend John Roget, Romilly wrote that the objection to the death penalty, founded on the errors of human tribunals and the impossibility of having absolute demonstration of the guilt of a criminal, struck him more forcibly than any argument he had ever heard before on the same side of the question. However, he confessed he thought it impossible to end the death penalty for all cases particularly since it was not the worst of punishments. Presumably, like some others including John Stuart Mill, he believed a long sentence of imprisonment or transportation would be worse. Nonetheless, he saw the laws of England as written in blood and more widely he subsequently declared that capital laws formed a kind of standard of cruelty to justify a harsh and excessive exercise of authority. Thus they became obstacles to social progress and also tended to increase the scale of other punishments.

Later, on 15 February 1816, Romilly was to introduce a Bill to repeal the Shoplifting Act which punished with death the crime of privately stealing in shops to the amount of five shillings and this was passed in the Commons.[5] It was rejected, however, by the House of Lords and caused Romilly to write a protest in which he expressed his dismay at the rejection:

> First, because the statute proposed to be repealed, which appoints the punishment of death for the offence of stealing, without violence or any circumstance of aggravation, property of a very small amount, is a law of excessive severity, is ill-suited to the character of the nation, and is repugnant to the spirit of our holy religion.
>
> Secondly, because to ordain the same punishment for crimes of the greatest atrocity and for offences which are low in the scale of moral guilt tends to confound all notions of justice, and to diminish the horror which crimes of the deepest dye ought to inspire.
>
> Thirdly, because the excessive severity of laws prevents the execution of them, and, by affording in many instances complete impunity to offenders, has a tendency to increase instead of preventing crimes. Fourthly, because by the alteration which has taken place in the value of money since the state of King William passed, it has become a law of much greater severity than was ever intended by the Legislature which passed it.[6]

Severity

Within two year of becoming a barrister, Romilly encountered the demand of the Reverend Martin Madan that the "sanguinary and barbarous penal code" should be rigidly enforced in every instance. Madan was himself a barrister, a Surrey magistrate and a cousin of William Cowper. He demanded

---

5. *Ibid.* p. 233.
6. *Ibid.* pp. 248-9.

an end to all reprieves and pardons so that severity could act as an effective deterrent in preventing crimes. Severity, he asserted, produced fear and made an example of the guilty. He dedicated his pamphlet setting out his proposals, called *Thoughts on Executive Justice,* to the judges of Assizes and sent each of them a copy.[7] Romilly was appalled by the folly, absurdity and inhumanity it displayed and at its apparent success in producing a bloodbath as a result of its influence on the judges. He wrote that whilst in the year before the work was published only 53 felons were executed in London, in the year following its publication the number had risen to 97 including the new spectacle of nearly 20 criminals at a time.[8]

Romilly was stung to reply to Madan with an essay entitled, *Observations on a late Publication Intituled, Thoughts on Executive Justice.*[9] He too then sent a copy to each of the judges, maintaining in the essay that imprisonment – then little used for criminals except on remand – was an appropriate and adequate substitute for the death penalty in most cases. The book had the distinction of being translated into French but, significantly, it was banned by the Paris police.

Following in the footsteps of Beccaria, Romilly argued that if the legislature provided for any crime a punishment more severe than was necessary to prevent that crime's commission, it was the author of unnecessary evil. And, unusually for the time, Romilly saw the principal aim of punishment as being the reformation of the criminal. The verdict he came to was that the excessive severity of the criminal law, far from acting as a deterrent as Madan claimed, was the principle cause of the increase in crime. As a consequence, he called for the majority of capital crimes to be revised.

Madan had further asserted that the rigour of the criminal laws was extremely beneficial. Hence, the punishment of the law should be executed relentlessly in every case without relaxation. Romilly considered that this view, "breathes a spirit contrary to the genius of the present times". Madan's doctrine, he wrote, "was not supported by dispassionate argument; instead

---

7. Martin Madan. (1785) *Thoughts on Executive Justice.* London, J. Dodsley.
8. Sir Samuel Romilly. (1842) *Memoirs of the Life of Sir Samuel Romilly Written by Himself and* edited by *his sons. Op. cit.* vol. i. p. 89.
9. Sir Samuel Romilly. (1786) *Observations on a late Publication Intituled Thoughts on Executive Justice by Martin Madan with a letter by Benjamin Franklin on the same subject.* London.

he uses far-fetched hyperboles, ferocious language, all the most specious colourings of rhetoric" and "at one time artfully and eloquently summoning to his aid the fears of his timid readers, and at another kindling the rage and indignation of what he calls the "poor oppressed, and innocent public".

Judicial Discretion

Whilst still only a young man, Romilly made a close study of the criminal law and began to practise more and more at Quarter Sessions where he found himself more frequently instructed than at Assizes. He also did battle with William Paley, M.A., D.D., Archdeacon of Carlisle who took a different approach to punishments from that of Madan. Paley, although not a lawyer, was intellectually more formidable than Madan. He seems to have arrived at his philosophy of penal law simply by regularly listening to cases at the Old Bailey and serving as a justice of the peace. Yet, in an amazing chapter of his book, *Principles of Moral and Political Philosophy*,[10] he gave to the practice of judicial discretion an ideological blessing that was to have a profound influence for nearly a century. At least to his own satisfaction, he disposed of the need for justice by saying that it was a dispensation to be expected only at the hand of God. On earth, he wrote, "the proper end of human punishment is not the satisfaction of justice but the prevention of crimes" even if the innocent suffered.

The eighteenth century landed aristocracy greatly approved, and were the beneficiaries, of the flexibility of the English criminal law. In the main they were able to defend themselves and their property with armed retainers when occasion arose but, in addition, they obtained a considerable degree of obedience and security from the legitimacy this discretionary nature of the penal law conferred on their rule. As justices of the peace in petty sessions and Quarter Sessions they were able both to operate the law and use its discretion to their advantage. With the fresh winds of Beccaria's condemnation of harsh penal laws and his humanistic alternative ringing around their ears

---

10. William Paley. (1785) *Principles of Moral and Political Philosophy*. London, T. & J. Allman. vol. ix, p. 526.

they were fortunate to have a noteworthy champion alight on the scene in the person of the archdeacon.

As early as 1470, in his *De Laudibus,* Fortescue had declared as a principle of criminal law, "I would rather wish twentie evil doers to escape death through pitie than one man be unjustly condemned". This was perhaps the first vague expression of the presumption of innocence. In relation to felony Blackstone was to confirm in his *Commentaries* the principle that the law holds that it is better that ten guilty persons escape than that one innocent suffer. Paley, in his much admired and influential book, published in 1785, would not have agreed. The death of an innocent person, he wrote, could not be placed in competition with the security of civil life which had to be protected by fear of punishment. The courts should reflect that he who fell by a mistaken sentence might be considered as falling for his country.

This stirred Romilly to great anger and a devastating response. The escape of ten guilty criminals was no trivial ill, he replied, "but it is less destructive of the security and happiness of the community than that one innocent man should be put to death. When guilty men escape, the law has merely failed but when an innocent man is condemned, it does great harm and creates a sense of insecurity in the population at large". He accused Paley of acting the patriot for others, and all his humanitarian instincts were aroused when he described the devastating consequences not only to the executed man, but for his equally innocent wife and children whose lives would be lived out in misery and ignominy.

With judicial discretion only two methods of applying the penal law were perceived by Paley. First, to provide capital punishment for few offences and invariably inflict it. Secondly, to utilize such punishment for many different kinds of offences, but inflict it upon only a few examples of each kind. He favoured the second approach. If death were reserved for one or two species of crime only, he argued, the most dangerous crimes would occur and not be punished in the manner that public safety required. Worse still, it would be known in advance that such crimes might be committed without danger to the offender's life.

To Paley's mind the law of England was constructed on a better policy. By the very large number of statutes creating capital offences the law swept into the net every crime which, under any circumstances might merit death.

But when the execution of the sentence was considered, a small proportion of each class was singled out where their general character, or the peculiar aggravations of their crimes, rendered them fit examples of public justice. By means of this danger of death hanging over the crimes of many, "the tenderness of the law cannot be taken advantage of".

This doctor of divinity was thus able to see from the "wisdom and humanity" of his design ample reason for a multiplicity of capital offences which, he explained, involved no cruelty since such laws were never meant to be executed indiscriminately. Nevertheless, frequent capital executions would still be required because of the increase in crime he saw arising from our liberty, our ever-expanding metropolitan cities, and the lack of an alternative punishment possessing sufficient terror.

As Professor Radzinowicz has said, it is impossible to over-estimate the importance of Paley's book, "which for many years exercised a potent influence on the trend of English criminal legislation".[11] Another writer observed that the book "reigned widely in England for near half a century, as the best modern work on ethical science".[12] In the House of Lords, Lord Ellenborough defended and followed Paley's doctrine consistently, and his book was adopted as a textbook by Cambridge University and ran through fifteen editions in his own lifetime.

Paley stood out for more judicial discretion in the criminal law which suited the landed gentry of the time. Romilly, on the other hand, believed the discretion of the judges made the criminal law unpredictable and considered that there was a wide difference "between investing the judges with the power to determine the degree in which the same species of punishment may be inflicted, and leaving it dependent on their will whether the offender shall be put to death, or shall only suffer a six months' imprisonment". He considered existing practice to be "a lottery of justice" and wanted to see more rule-bound law within the general context of the rule of law.

In 1798 Romilly married Anne, daughter of Francis Garbett of Knill Court, Herefordshire and, with his practice as a barrister flourishing, in the

---

11. Leon Radzinowicz. (1948) *A History of English Criminal Law and its Administration from 1750: The Movement for Reform.* London, Stevens & Sons Limited. vol. i. pp. 248-9.
12. Professor T.R. Birks. (1874) *Modern Utilitarianism.* London, Macmillan & Co. p. 48.

year 1800 he was appointed King's Counsel. This was followed in 1805 by his appointment as Chancellor of the County Palatine of Durham.

Parliamentary Crusade

Many of Romilly's activities in supporting the rule of law occurred in a period of industrial and political unrest. Economic distress was widespread, repression was common and at one point *habeas corpus* was suspended. Spies and informers were to be found everywhere to penetrate organizations of the growing working-class which was becoming radicalised. In the period that preceded the violence of the movement for the Reform Bill of 1831 capital laws were frequently used to stifle dissent.

In the early stages of this period, Romilly found himself attracted in politics to the Whig party and on 8 February 1806 he was offered the post of Solicitor-General in the Grenville "Ministry of All the Talents" although he was not an MP. He accepted the offer and was quickly knighted (against his inclination, he said, but the King insisted) and entered the House of Commons as the Member for the borough of Queensborough unopposed. His first task was to attend the Privy Council to examine a case in which three British seamen had been flogged to death at Bombay in 1801. He found that it was not uncommon for officers to inflict very severe punishments under the impression that they had the legal power to do so.

Romilly felt so strongly that this was wrong that he spoke to the First Lord of the Admiralty about it in order to prevent it happening in the future, but nothing was done. Accordingly, he was to return to the matter time and time again being appalled at the number of deaths in the army and navy arising from the torture of suffering 1,000 (or sometimes 1,500) lashes, often for the most trivial offences. And, later, on 8 March 1815, he moved in the Commons to add to the Mutiny Bill a clause to restrict the maximum number of lashes to 100. He withdrew the motion only on being assured that floggings had rarely been inflicted lately and a promise that the question would be examined with a view to lessening the severity of corporal punishments and, if possible, to abolish them entirely.

He also agreed, at the request of William Wilberforce, to speak in the House in support of any measure to abolish the slave trade. He fulfilled his promise on June 10 on a motion by Charles James Fox that the trade be abolished. Romilly took the stand that it had long been decided that the trade should go on the basis of evidence that it was carried on by robbery, rape and murder and that it was time it went. He may have been heartened that his speech gave grave offence to the MP for Liverpool, a port well-known to slave traders, and to some others.

In spite of being involved in many varied matters which came before the Commons, Romilly is best remembered as an MP for constantly introducing Bills to mitigate the harshness of the penal laws and in showing great perseverance in the face of widespread and powerful opposition from judges and in the House of Lords. However, he had a great deal of public support including from magazines such as the *Monthly Review* and the *Quarterly Review*. As part of his belief in the rule of law he also strongly criticised the dilatory Assize process under which a person might lie in prison for eight months or more before being brought to trial. Indeed, he complained that in the North of England delays were often up to a year, and in Hull, three years.

By this time Romilly's early attack on Madan had developed into a more mature penal theory. This he fully expressed in a brilliant speech to the House of Commons on 9 February 1810, when moving for leave to bring into the House three Bills to repeal certain statutes imposing the death penalty for larceny. This was published, with some additions, as a pamphlet entitled, *Observations on the Criminal Law of England as it relates to Capital Punishments, and on the Mode in which it is administered*.[13] It was enthusiastically praised by Brougham in an article in the *Edinburgh Review* as "a beautiful and interesting tract".[14]

Romilly denied that the exercise of discretion in the execution of the laws could produce a regular, mature and well-digested system. On the contrary, he stressed the importance of certainty and asked how it could be said that the species of punishment was clearly determined for every offence, when, in practice, it was for the judge to say whether a criminal was to suffer death,

---

13. Sir Samuel Romilly. (1820) *Speeches in the House of Commons*. London, vol. i. pp. 108-194.
14. *Edinburgh Review*. (1811-12) vol. ixx. pp. 389-415.

transportation or imprisonment. If punishments were really certain, then they could be very light indeed.

In the case of all capital felonies based upon the value of goods stolen, Romilly believed that inflation should be taken into account and the laws re-enacted to ensure that the sums involved, such as theft to a value of twelve pence or more, should be revised substantially upwards. As all the articles of life, he said, had been gradually for many years becoming dearer, the life of man has, in the view of the legislature, been growing cheaper and of less account.

On 22 June 1815, Romilly intervened in the debate on a Bill to continue both the system of transportation, and imprisonment on the hulks, generally and without limit. He opposed both and particularly the confining of prisoners in the rotting and decayed floating prisons which had been described as a "Hell on Earth". Romilly pointed out that instead of reforming offenders, the hulks only made them more depraved and more dangerous to society. Returns made to the Commons revealed that "there is one boy in the hulks who is only 11 years old, two of whom are only 12, one who is only 13 and four who are 14 and altogether, no fewer than 112 who are under the age of 20".[15] The bad effects of the country's punishments, he said, were shown by the fact that the number of persons committed for trial at the Old Bailey had risen from 899 in the year 1806 to 1,413 in 1814.[16]

Romilly exposed in great detail both the defects and the contradictions of the criminal law and their harmful consequences. He discussed at length, and in Benthamite terms, the concept of punishments and made impassioned pleas for reform backed by the many Bills he endeavoured to steer through Parliament. On procedure, he wanted the accused to be made competent to give evidence, grand juries to examine those bringing charges and justices of the peace to deal summarily with minor offences. He wanted parties and witnesses to be compensated for their trouble and loss of time, as well as reparation made to those found not guilty.

---

15. Sir Samuel Romilly. *Memoirs of the Life of Sir Samuel Romilly Written by Himself and edited by his sons. Op. cit.* vol. iii, pp. 184-5.
16. *Ibid.* p. 185.

Romilly's Bills, although well supported, were defeated largely because the bishops combined with Lord Chancellor Eldon and Lord Chief Justice Ellenborough in opposing them in the House of Lords. In expectation of this he had declined to consult the judges before introducing his Bills. Lord Ellenborough, in particular, was bitterly hostile to any change in the criminal law on the ground that it was sanctified by its antiquity. In attacking a Bill to abolish the pillory, he held up its ancient origin as a merit and took occasion to declaim against any innovation in the criminal law. Romilly asked his Lordship and other opponents of reform whether, had they lived some time before they would have been in favour of such "bulwarks of the Constitution" as disembowelling alive or the burning of women alive for felony, and whether the removal of those "bulwarks" had endangered the Constitution.

If any person desired, wrote Romilly, to have an adequate idea of the mischievous effects produced in England by the French Revolution and all its attendant horrors, he should attempt some legislative reform on humane and liberal principles. He will then find, he added, not only what a stupid dread of innovation but what a savage spirit it has put into the minds of many of his countrymen. And he instanced a young man who was the brother of a peer who said, "I am against your Bill... There is no good done by mercy. They only get worse; I would hang them all up at once".

Writing of the opposition of the Archbishop of Canterbury and other named bishops to a Bill to abolish the punishment of death for the crime of stealing to the value of five shillings in a shop, he said in his *Memoirs*:

> I rank these prelates amongst the members who were solicited to vote against the Bill, because I would rather be convinced of their servility towards government, than that, recollecting the mild doctrines of their religion, they could have come down to the House spontaneously, to vote that transportation for life is not a sufficiently severe punishment for the offence of pilfering what is of five shillings' value, and that nothing but the blood of the offender can afford an adequate atonement for such a transgression.[17]

He said that the argument principally relied upon by those who spoke against the Bill was that innovations in the criminal law were dangerous. He was

---

17. Vol.ii, p. 331.

attacked for that reason. He had been the author of the Act, passed two years before, to abolish the punishment of death for the crime of picking pockets and that had resulted in a great increase in crime. But how did they know that crime had increased? All they could know was that prosecutions were much more frequent than before the Act was passed. Instead of giving any argument against the Act, it proves its efficiency.

It was stated, when the Bill was proposed, he continued, that the severity of the punishment prevented those who had been robbed from prosecuting. Take the severe punishment away, it was said, and there would be many more prosecutions. The punishment was taken away, many more prosecutions followed, and this was the very fact that these men, blinded by gross prejudices, put forward to show the measure had been unsuccessful. On the contrary, it was the strongest proof of its success. It would have been seen as a triumph if we had been capable of enjoying it.[18]

In the face of such opposition it is remarkable that Romilly did achieve some successes. By persistently, time and again, introducing into the Commons Bills to reform the criminal law, he secured the enactment of six statutes to remove the death penalty from certain crimes and his speeches made a deep and lasting impression in the country at large, as well as in Parliament. The driving force behind his energy in the cause of reform was outstanding. He undoubtedly played a crucial part in the growth of the movement for reducing the incidence of the death penalty and reforming the barbaric criminal law. His arguments were to recur again and again in the speeches and proposals of the great criminal law reformers who followed him as well as in the Reports of the Criminal Law Commissioners.

Conclusion

Romilly died by his own hand in his house in Russell Square, London on 2 November 1818, just three days after the death of his beloved wife on the Isle of Wight. His anxiety during her illness preyed upon his mind and affected his health and the shock of her death caused his own. His mantle

---

18. *Ibid.* pp. 332-3.

was immediately taken up by Fowell Buxton, and by Sir James Mackintosh who secured the appointment of the *Select Committee of Inquiry into the State of the Criminal Law.* They, in turn, were later to make way for Sir Robert Peel who, as Home Secretary, finally secured the repeal of the notorious Waltham Black Act, the ending of capital punishment for certain kinds of larceny, and a number of other important reforms. Eventually, during the course of 1837, and as a consequence of his inspiration, Lord John Russell secured the removal of the death penalty from 21 of the 37 offences still capital with restrictions on the use of such punishment for the 16 remaining. Soon the death penalty was to be inflicted only in the cases of murder and treason and imprisonment became the principal punishment for felony. Romilly's aims were at last achieved and his insistence on the rule of law vindicated.

As one writer has put it, although the struggle for reform was to be a long one, Romilly made it "infinitely easier for the generation coming after him to dispel the old errors, prejudices and tyrannies, to shake off the bondage of noxious traditions and to introduce in criminal law numerous salutary changes of an almost revolutionary nature". [19]

---

19. Coleman Phillipson. (1923) *Three Criminal Law Reformers, Beccaria, Bentham, Romilly.* London, J.M. Dent & Sons. p. 332.

CHAPTER 10

SIR WILLIAM GARROW

"Billingsgate Boy"

A startling fact about William Garrow is that he was airbrushed out of history. His successes and his key role in changing the face of the English criminal trial and related procedures became a lost story. The reasons for this are open to conjecture. There are, however, strong indications of what accounts for it.

Garrow was born the son of a schoolmaster in 1760; not really part of respectable society according to the temper of the times. Furthermore, in adult life, in order to be successful in undermining the evidence perjuring thief-takers who prosecuted in return for blood money, he had to be aggressive, and even brash, in court. This did wonders for his reputation with prisoners, juries and the public but it did not endear him to fellow barristers and judges who often appreciated manners above integrity and ability. They claimed he was ignorant of the law and despised his instinctive knowledge of human nature and feeling for the common man. As a consequence they condescendingly referred to him as the "the Billingsgate Boy".

A third reason may stem from the bad reputation of the Old Bailey itself and of those few barristers who practised there, when prisoners were largely denied the assistance of counsel, as Garrow did for ten years from 1783 to 1793. They were generally considered to be disreputable thugs and bullies. According to Allyson N May they were widely regarded, inside and outside the profession, as "old Bailey hacks" and dishonest ruffians exercising low standards of advocacy.[1] And, calling for reform at the Old Bailey in 1834, *The Times* newspaper in an editorial complained of barristers there being "veteran brawlers and bullies" who were "irritable and foul-mouthed". For good measure it added that, "The Old Bailey has long been a scandal to the

---

1. Allyson N May. (2003) *The Bar and the Old Bailey, 1750-1850.* Chapel Hill and London, The University of North Carolina Press.

country, and a by-word expressive of everything coarse and indecent in the business of advocacy".[2]

Not that these descriptions fitted Garrow. But could this low image of the court explain why eminent jurists such as Sir William Blackstone, Sir William Holdsworth, James Fitzjames Stephen, Leon Radzinowicz, James Bradley Thayer and others, including members of the Bar, all failed to see the significance of Garrow or the birth of adversary trial and right for prisoners for which he was so largely responsible? Stephen was the only one to mention the change towards adversariality but failed to see how it had arisen. He wrote:

> The *most remarkable change* into the practice of the courts [in the eighteenth century] was the process by which the old rule which deprived prisoners of the assistance of counsel in trials for felony was gradually relaxed. A practice sprung up, *the growth of which cannot now be traced*, by which counsel were allowed to do everything for prisoners accused of felony except addressing the jury for them.[3]

Stephen was not entirely accurate, however, since counsel were not allowed to make speeches or examine their clients, see the Indictment before the commencement of the trial or take instructions from their clients in prison. Nor were prisoners or their witnesses permitted to give evidence on oath. So the rules were stacked against the prisoner and makes Garrow's achievement in destroying them, and the ignorance about him, even more remarkable.

From just after Garrow's death on 24 September 1840 it was as if he had not existed – until the year 1991. The rediscovery of the significance of Garrow was led by John Beattie who published an article entitled "Garrow for the Defence" in the February 1991 issue of *History Today*.[4] This was followed by Beattie's "Scales of Justice: Defence Counsel and the English Criminal Trial in the Eighteenth and Nineteenth Centuries" in the October 1991 issue of *Law and History Review* which outlined the new courtroom style

---

2. *The Times.* (4 November 1834) p. 2.
3. Italics added by the author of this work. James Fitzjames Stephen. (1883) *A History of the Criminal Law of England.* London, Macmillan, vol. i, p. 424.
4. J.M. Beattie. (1991) "Garrow for the Defence". *History Today.* History Today Limited.

pursued by Garrow.⁵ In 2003, John H Langbein published his *The Origins of Adversary Criminal Trial* in which he devotes a good deal of space to the Old Bailey although he is opposed to adversary trial and considers Garrow to have been a "trickster".⁶

However, as Geoffrey Robertson QC has written:

> [Garrow] was certainly no "trickster" as Langbein mistakenly labelled him, but rather an advocate who came into court equipped with savage wit, a fearless capacity to object to unfair evidence, and clever tactics.⁷

The first book to deal at length with Garrow and the trials in which he was involved was *Fighting for Justice: The History and Origins of Adversary Trial*, published in 2006. It contained chapters explaining Garrow's revolutionary impact on criminal law and procedure and the world-wide influence which this had. Finally came the 2010 work written with Richard Braby, a direct descendant of William Garrow, under the title *Sir William Garrow: His Life, Times and Fight for Justice* which adds a great deal of new legal and genealogical information.⁸ This book includes detailed extracts from many of Garrow's trials and his importance in legal history is now more fully recognised. Indeed, it provides an invaluable "missing link" for legal and social historians. It also gives fresh information about Garrow and his family based upon Richard's 20 years of research. Now on the Internet there is a website entitled "The Garrow Society" on which are a host of fascinating items about Garrow. These include extracts from some of his most famous trials; a glimpse into the mystery of his wife Sarah; information and photographs of his cliff-top villa in Kent and its blue plaque; details of the Sarah

---

5. J.M. Beattie. (1991) "Scales of Justice: Defence Counsel and the English Criminal Trial in the Eighteenth and Nineteenth Centuries". 9(2) *Law and History Review*. University of Illinois Press.
6. John H. Langbein. (2003) *The Origins of Adversary Criminal Trial*. Oxford, Oxford University Press.
7. Geoffrey Robertson QC. (2010). Foreword to Hostettler and Braby's *Sir William Garrow: His Life Times and Fight for Justice*, Waterside Press, p. xiv.
8. John Hostettler. (2006) *Fighting for Justice: The History and Origins of Adversary Trial*. Winchester, Waterside Press and John Hostettler and Richard Braby. (2010) *Sir William Garrow: His Life, Times and Fight for Justice*. Hook, Hampshire. Waterside Press.

Dore Detective Club and William Garrow in the British Museum as well as many other items of interest.

Old Bailey Practice and Changing the Law

Garrow was born in Middlesex on 13 April 1760. He was admitted by Lincoln's Inn on 27 November 1778 and called to the Bar on 27 November 1783 when he commenced criminal practice at the Old Bailey. Earlier in the century prisoners charged with felony (which meant most crimes and was punishable with death) could not have counsel appear for them at all, except on points of law with the permission of the judge, following a ruling in a case of rape in the reign of King Edward I in the thirteenth century.[9] This was because in English criminal law indictments for felony were taken, and still are, in the name of the Monarch (a fiction used initially to augment the King's income) and in early times it was considered *lèse majesté* for those indicted to be allowed counsel to appear against the King or Queen. Later, jurists including Coke argued that the no-counsel rule was justified because the judge acted as counsel for the prisoner. In reality, however, whilst some judges might ensure that a prisoner was treated fairly that was by no means always the case. At the same time the prisoner could not give evidence on oath or call witnesses to do so on his behalf.

But with the Treason Trials Act 1696,[10] the situation was changed for those accused in state trials. Prisoners charged with high treason were permitted to engage counsel to act for them although this was not extended to trials for felony. For centuries the judges resolutely enforced the prohibition on defence counsel in cases of felony, despite persistent complaints by defendants.[11] Indeed, it was pointed out with some alarm by a judge in a trial in 1602, that if counsel were allowed in that case, "every prisoner would want it".[12] Even Lord Chief Justice Jeffreys, known as the "hanging judge" for his brutality in court, told Thomas Rosewall on a charge of high treason in 1684,

---

9. *Year Books*. 30 and 31, Edw. I. (Rolls Series) pp. 520-30.
10. 7 & 8 Wm. III, c. 3.
11. John H. Langbein. *The Origins of Adversary Criminal Trial. Op. cit.* pp. 10-11.
12. R. v. Boothe. (1602) British Library. *Add. Mss.* 25203. f569v. Cited by J.H. Baker. (1979) *An*

> I think it is a harsh case that a man should have counsel to defend himself for a two-penny-trespass [a misdemeanour] and his witnesses examined on oath; but if he steal, commit murder or felony, nay, high treason, where life, estate, honour, and all are concerned, he shall neither have counsel, nor his witnesses examined on oath.[13]

Savage Cross-Examination

By the time when Garrow started practice at the Old Bailey in 1783 prisoners were occasionally allowed by some judges to have counsel to briefly cross-examine prosecution witnesses but nothing more, and only a few took advantage of this discretionary move. Furthermore, there were few rules of evidence and counsel were not permitted to make speeches or address the jury. Crucially, there was no presumption of innocence. A usually uneducated prisoner had to prove his innocence if he could in the daunting atmosphere of the courtroom and its procedures. It was in 1791 that Garrow was the first counsel to express the presumption of innocence clearly in an English court.[14] During the trial of George Dingler for murder, he told the judge that it should be "recollected by all the bystanders (for you do not require to be reminded of it) that every man is presumed to be innocent till proved guilty".[15] Nevertheless, the principle was not widely accepted at the time and prisoners did not have the benefit of other rules of evidence such as the rules against hearsay and involuntary confessions, the right to silence, and the rule against self-incrimination.

Garrow was to change all that. Under the law of the time individuals were paid a sum of £40 by the government for each person they accused of a criminal offence who was found guilty. This led to numerous "thief-takers" who would commit perjury and prosecute innocent men, women

---

Introduction to Legal History. London, Butterworths, p. 417.
13. 10 Howell's *State Trials.* col. 267.
14. Many years later Sir Edward Marshall Hall was to depict the figure of Justice holding the scales until the presumption of innocence helped turn the scales in favour of the prisoner.
15. OBP Online. (www.oldbaileyonline.org. 8 August 2010) 14 September 1791. Trial of George Dingler for Murder. Ref: t17910914-1.

and children for the money (a substantial sum at the time) which became known as "blood money" since the accused people who were found guilty of felony faced death on the gallows. As a consequence juries did not suffer thief-takers gladly and Garrow used all his powers and personal knowledge of many of them to expose them by devastating cross-examination. Criminal trials were conducted in a taproom atmosphere with counsel, judges, jurors and members of the public all joining in the rumbustious fray as portrayed in the BBC series 'Garrow's Law'.[16]

In his ten years at the Old Bailey Garrow fought nearly 1,000 trials and revolutionised the practice of criminal law. Here, in the Assize court for London and Middlesex, one can see a mirror-image of the crime-ridden side of the city as felons and innocents pass before through the court charged with murder, robbery and shoplifting. Garrow's savage cross-examination of bounty-hunters who perjured themselves for blood money became an example to his contemporaries at the Old Bailey and brought him increasing numbers of clients as well as substantial fees. May has shown that an upper limit of roughly six per cent of prisoners at the Old Bailey were represented by counsel in the middle of the eighteenth century and that this had risen to 28 per cent by 1800.[17] Forbidden to address the jury, Garrow managed to approach them obliquely through his cross-examination. At the same time he and other defence barristers kept up the pressure for rules of evidence to assist prisoners and eventually persuaded the judges, one by one, to allow them.

Adversary Trial and the Rule of Law

Garrow's career as counsel was distinguished and he was the first to establish a public reputation as a criminal barrister.[18] As such he left an indelible mark on the style of adversary trial that lives on today. He used simple language and never lectured jurors or spoke down to them. His importance lies in the fact that he was the first to develop the techniques and skills of adversary

---

16. 1 November 2009 onwards. BBC1.
17. Allyson N. May. *The Bar and the Old Bailey, 1750-1850, Op. cit.* pp. 29 and 34.
18. D. Lemmings. (2000) *Professors of the Law: Barristers and English Legal Culture in the Eighteenth Century.* Oxford, Oxford University Press, p. 211.

trial and in doing so change the nature of the trial and enhance the rule of law. In all, Garrow appeared in more than 961 trials at the Old Bailey and in three-quarters of them he was counsel for the defence. In the year 1786 alone he acted in 117 of the 182 trials in which counsel were named in the reported cases, which is a remarkable record.

Adversary trial, which Garrow did so much to establish, is part of the fabric of the rule of law. And, "it is not unreasonable to link the birth of adversariality with the more profound shifts in contemporary understanding of the world and the political economy which followed from the Glorious Revolution of 1688".[19] For the prisoner in the dock charged with felony and weighed down by rules that, unless the jury showed mercy and committed "pious perjury", or he had "benefit of clergy",[20] meant his life was in serious danger. The change to adversary trial was a momentous transformation. It was part of the process whereby the lawyers captured the courtroom and radically changed the criminal trial and broke down the judges' mastery of the proceedings. In addition, defence counsel exploited the art of cross-examination and legal argument to challenge suspect evidence that might unduly influence jurors, such as hearsay, confessions and the evidence of thief-takers and accomplices testifying under the promise of immunity from prosecution. And, Garrow was the pioneer in using cross-examination as a means to comment on the evidence in frequent asides to the jury and to refute or discredit the prosecution case and battle aggressively for the accused.

Adversary trial reached its height with the Prisoners' Counsel Act of 1836,[21] which finally allowed defence counsel to address the jury, and the Criminal Evidence Act 1898, which permitted prisoners to give evidence on oath.[22] And, it not only flourished in England but was widely and quickly adopted in other countries where it had a vital impact on criminal procedure around the globe. In the process it also played a critical part in enhancing the concept of due process of law. It was England's gift to the world.

---

19. Richard Vogler. (2005) *A World View of Criminal Justice*. Aldershot, Ashgate Publishing Limited. pp. 142-3.
20. A device whereby a convicted felon would be set free if he or she could read the first verse of psalm 51 (the so-called "neck verse"). It was not abolished until 1837.
21. 6 and 7 Will. IV. c. 114.
22. 62. Vict. c. 36.

Adversary trial was in direct contrast to the Roman-canon inquisitorial system in operation in other parts of the world including continental Europe. Differing from the battle between opposing counsel in adversary trial, the continental system imposed on the judge a duty to enquire into the circumstances of a case with a view to uncovering the truth. In fact, his powers were so extensive that his authority had to be limited by evidentiary strictures under which, according to Stephan Landsman:

> He could convict a criminal defendant in only two circumstances: when two eye witnesses were produced who had observed the gravamen of the crime, or when the defendant confessed. Circumstantial evidence was never sufficient in itself to warrant conviction. These evidentiary rules made it impossible to obtain convictions in many cases unless the defendant was willing to confess. Roman-canon process authorised the use of torture to extract the necessary confessions. Thus, torture became a tool of judicial inquiry and was used to generate the evidence upon which the defendant would be condemned.[23]

In England, criminal procedure made the prosecution and the defence responsible for producing all the evidence on which a jury would base its verdict. In time, it was this conflict between the parties that would enable barristers like Garrow to build adversary trial and rules of criminal evidence.

Human Rights

Adversary trial and trial by jury were incorporated into the American Bill of Rights on the initiative of Thomas Jefferson. And, ultimately the legal rights of individual defendants in criminal trials was recognised in Europe with article 6 of the Convention for the Protection of Human Rights and Fundamental Freedoms[24] which was incorporated into United Kingdom domestic law by the Human Rights Act 1998, c. 42. With echoes of Dicey's definition of the rule of law, article 6(1) provides a general right to a fair and

---

23. S. Landsman. (1983) "A Brief Survey of the Development of the Adversary System". 44(1) *Ohio State Law Journal*. p. 724.
24. www.hri.org/docsECHR50.html

public trial by an independent court of law and also sets out other minimum rights. Article 6(3)(d) states that, "everyone charged with a criminal offence has the following minimum rights ... to examine, or have examined, witnesses against him". Although it is not always recognised as such, it is clear that adversary trial is a basic ingredient of the rule of law.

The right to cross-examine witnesses is an intrinsic part of the Anglo-American adversary system of trial and the wonder of it is that it was born in England not by legislation but by the practical efforts of Garrow and other barristers in their concern not with developing the law but simply to win cases by the best means available. That they did so in the favourable environment of an expanding concept of the rule of law and of a human rights culture in no way diminishes their achievement. And, at last the crucial role of this intrepid lawyer has been brought into the public domain. No longer need jurists remain in the dark about the genesis of adversariality.

Assessment

Garrow died at his country home, Pegwell Cottage near Ramsgate in Kent, on 24 September 1840. He was survived by a daughter, his wife and son having pre-deceased him.

He could not have been at all conscious that he was one of the prime architects of the adversary system of trial in the criminal courts. No mention of such a system passed his lips or those of any contemporary lawyers or jurists. Equally, it is clear from his remarks in court that he would have been only dimly aware that in his advocacy he also played a prominent part in securing the rules of evidence in criminal trials that helped make such trials fairer for defendants. In effect, he gave expression to the deep-rooted notion of opposing parties in the common law and the English psyche whereby lawyers champion opposing causes. And in modern times conflict has become a key social issue.

From his start at the Old Bailey, Garrow revealed his self-confidence and his aggressive and often ironic style when dealing with prosecution witnesses. He also showed an understanding of the law, which was often denied by his contemporaries, and a willingness to stand up to the judges when he thought this necessary. Over the years he was a major influence in turning cross-examination into an art form and a vital component in adversariality which itself changed the thrust of the criminal trial. Without counsel such as Garrow it is not clear that adversary trial would have come into being. Reports of Garrow's trials at the Old Bailey reveal him exerting his powers with the result that defence counsel became the dominant force in the courtroom and captured its mastery for the lawyers in place of the judge who was often influenced by politicians.

In the event, adversariality and the rules of evidence soon travelled to, and became rooted in, many parts of the world. Indeed, the process is still continuing. As a contributing factor in the establishment of a culture of human rights and as an integral part of the modern concept of the rule of law adversariality has had a large and lasting impact on world-wide jurisprudence. For the crucial part played in the drama of the birth of criminal defence advocacy by this intrepid lawyer from a humble background, his name shines forth like a beacon in the darkness.

CHAPTER II

CRIMINAL LAW COMMISSIONERS

Terror and Legitimacy

The Great Reform Act of 1832 was a watershed in the growth of democracy in Britain. The times saw a tide of new forces and ideas in the life of the nation that were to strengthen beyond measure the rule of law and the modern concept of human rights. In the years leading up to the Act, the country had been rent by tensions arising from the stark alternatives of squalor and prosperity on the one hand and violence and deference on the other. Such tensions had given rise to a frenzy for social, economic, cultural and political change. Under the influence of fears arising from the French Revolution British governments had for years blocked reform of the franchise, refused to alleviate distress following the end of the Napoleonic Wars and responded with violence and legal repression to any demand for reform. The Massacre at Peterloo, when, on 16 August 1819, the yeomanry attacked an 80,000 large peaceful, holiday-like demonstration at St. Peter's Fields, Manchester, was one example and the outlawing of trade unions by the Combination Laws of 1799 and 1800 was another.

The criminal law was woven around the death penalty which "formed an ugly apex to a system of social control through legal processes which functioned to a significant degree at the pleasure of the governors".[1] It was used both as a means of terror and of legitimacy by the landed squires and justices of the peace to preserve their society. And they were appalled to see that among many other instruments of their rule it was to be transformed by what were seen as the new ruling class in the nation. The desire for reform of the criminal law and its institutions was a crucial element in the ferment of ideas and movement for change that had followed in the wake of the

---

1. W.R. Cornish. (1978) "Criminal Justice and Punishment". In Cornish and Others. *Crime and Law in Nineteenth Century Britain*. Dublin, Irish Academic Press Ltd., p. 18.

Glorious Revolution of 1689 and the ongoing Industrial Revolution. Hence, in 1833 Lord Brougham, then at the height of his fame as an architect of the Reform Act, secured from William IV a Royal Commission to help sweep away the barbaric feudal relics that made up the law of crimes and replace them with new liberal-leaning codes.

The Criminal Law Commissioners

Five Commissioners were selected by Lord Chancellor Brougham for the task. They were Andrew Amos, Henry Bellenden Ker, Thomas Starkie, William (afterwards Mr. Justice) Wightman and John Austin. Their task was awesome but there can be no doubt they were eminently suitable for it. All were distinguished, liberal law reformers and as the Whig *Edinburgh Review* commented: "It certainly would not be easy to find anywhere men better fitted for the satisfactory discharge of the important duty committed to them".[2]

Andrew Amos
Andrew Amos was born in 1791 in India where his father on his travels had married the daughter of a Swiss officer. He was educated at Eton and Trinity College Cambridge and called to the Bar by Middle Temple. He served successively as Recorder of Oxford, Nottingham and Banbury and on the foundation of the University of London became its first professor of English law with John Austin, appointed professor of jurisprudence, as his colleague. Between the years 1829 and 1837 his lectures attained great celebrity. In the latter year he was appointed law member of the Governor-General's Council in India in succession to Lord Macaulay. He stood, unsuccessfully as a Whig Parliamentary candidate for Hull in 1832. He died on 18 April 1860.

Henry Bellenden Ker
Henry Bellenden Ker was born in about 1785. He was called to the Bar by Lincoln's Inn and was active in promoting Parliamentary reform prior to the Reform Act. He was elected a Fellow of the Royal Society in 1819 but

---
2. *Edinburgh Review*. (1837) vol. 65. p. 214.

resigned in 1830, unable to tolerate the election of a royal Duke as President in preference to Sir John Herschel, the distinguished astronomer.[3] He wrote many books and sat on the 1854 Royal Commission which led to the Statute Law Revision Acts and later the Criminal Law Consolidation Acts of 1861. He stood, unsuccessfully, as a Whig parliamentary candidate for Norwich. In 1860, at the age of seventy-five, he retired to a villa near Brougham's at Cannes and died on 2 November 1871.

Thomas Starkie

Thomas Starkie was born in Blackburn, Lancashire on 12 April 1782. He graduated with an MA at St. John's College, Cambridge in 1806 and followed his father in being senior wrangler and 1st Smith's prizeman, a unique double. He was called to the Bar, also by Lincoln's Inn, on 23 May 1810. Like, and preceding, Amos he was elected Downing Professor of Laws at Cambridge and, in 1847, appointed a county court judge. Originally a Tory in politics he became a Whig and unsuccessfully contested Cambridge in the General Election of 1840. He wrote a number of treatises, his chief work being a *Practical Treatise on the Law of Evidence* (1824) in three volumes. All his books were highly regarded in the profession and ran into several editions in England and America. He died in his rooms in Downing College on 15 April 1849 whilst still an active member of the Criminal Law Commission.

William Wightman

William Wightman was born in 1784. He graduated with an MA at University College, Oxford on 23 October 1809. He entered Lincoln's Inn on 31 January 1804 and practised as a special pleader before being called to the Bar in 1821. He was engaged in many celebrated cases including the prosecutions arising out of the Bristol riots, and had a deep learning of the law. He became a junior counsel to the Treasury, and in February 1841 he was appointed a judge of the Queen's Bench whereupon he ceased his work as a member of the Royal Commission. He was nearly twenty-three years a judge and died, whilst on circuit, on 10 December 1863.

---

3. Sir Cecil Carr. (1955) *A Victorian Law Reformer's Correspondence*. London, Quaritch, p. 7.

John Austin

John Austin the celebrated jurist, was born on 3 March 1790. He was five years in the army before being called to the Bar in 1818 by the Inner Temple. Austin might have been expected to perform well as a member of the Criminal Law Commission but his wife, Sarah, wrote that he found the work uncongenial and came home disturbed and agitated from every meeting.[4] He thought the work of the Commission unduly expensive to a public who would gain little benefit from it. Perhaps he was biased since he told Sarah that he preferred the idea of drafting a criminal law code himself with a Commission then appointed "to pull it to pieces".[5] In any event, he resigned after the Commission's Second Report in 1836. Later he was to write that the consequences of any proposed Parliamentary reform would be entirely mischievous. After a happy but poor retirement he died in December 1859.

David Jardine

David Jardine, who replaced Austin on the Commission, was born at Pickwick, near Bath, in 1794. He graduated with an MA at Glasgow University in 1813 and was called to the Bar as a member of the Middle Temple on 7 February 1823. He was a writer on both historical and legal matters and combined the two in his *Reading on Torture*[6] which exposed the extensive cover-up of the use of torture by royal prerogative during the reign of the Tudors and early Stuarts. Jardine was also a practising barrister who became Recorder of Bath and in 1839 was appointed police magistrate at Bow Street in London. He died on 13 September 1860.

---

4. John Austin. (1861) Preface to *The Province of Jurisprudence Determined*. (1995 edition) Cambridge, Cambridge University Press.
5. *Ibid.*
6. David Jardine. (1836) *A Reading on the Use of Torture in the Criminal Law of England prior to the Commonwealth*. Delivered at New Inn Hall, Michaelmas Term 1836 and reprinted in the *Edinburgh Review* (April-July 1838), vol. 67.

Inspiration

The qualities and qualifications of these men cannot then be in doubt. They took intellectual inspiration from Jeremy Bentham and studied the classic achievements of Sir Edward Coke, Sir Matthew Hale and Beccaria as well as other criminal and penal law reformers. To Brougham they were all brilliant lawyers in their own fields, both practical and academic, and all had extensive learning. They shared similar educational backgrounds and professional interests and they all believed in the rule of law and the necessity for criminal law reform. With great enthusiasm they made a masterly attempt to bring the entire criminal law system into tune with the new times. They formed a coherent radical group and enhanced the humanitarian movement of the early nineteenth century by spearpointing the mitigation of the cruel criminal law in line with an extension of the rule of law. Their achievements, in securing the crucially important reforms in the criminal law required by their Whig patron, were remarkable.

Prisoners' Counsel Act

Having the right to be defended by counsel is a significant part of the rule of law and we find the Commissioners making a crucial contribution to the Prisoners' Counsel Act 1836. In spite of the heroic and successful efforts of William Garrow and others in the late eighteenth century to secure defence rights for prisoners, by 1830 counsel could still not fully represent prisoners on trial for felony. They continued to be confined to cross-examining prosecution witnesses and continued to be forbidden to make a speech or address the jury. From 1821 to 1834 both liberal and radical Members of Parliament had introduced Bills into the House of Commons to rectify this but they were all defeated, mainly in the House of Lords. Then, in 1836, William Ewart, the radical barrister MP for Liverpool, introduced yet another Bill. This passed the Commons with a large majority, but still faced the hostility of the lawyers and landed interests in the Lords.

Lord John Russell, who had been appointed Home Secretary in April 1835, was determined to break the deadlock. Despite the heavy workload of the Criminal Law Commissioners, he approached them to assist him secure enactment of Ewart's Bill. They agreed to do so and produced a powerful report in favour of full representation of prisoners charged with felony by defence counsel.[7] Russell had this published just prior to the decisive speech for the Bill in the House of Lords by Lord Lyndhurst. In the course of his speech, which relied heavily upon the Report, Lyndhurst described it as the Commissioners "most elaborate and learned report in favour of the Bill". The report covered every aspect of the question and Lyndhurst repeated many of the arguments which supported change. It deplored the existing law as a "remnant of a barbarous code of laws relating to felons".[8] And, for the first time for a Bill on this subject Lyndhurst was able with an able speech to gain the support of a majority of the peers. The Bill then speedily received the royal assent and passed into law.[9] With their report the Commissioners had made a substantial contribution to the rule of law under which all prisoners are entitled to a fair trial.

Death Penalty

Encouraged by this victory, Russell, in 1837, set about seeking the further support of the Commissioners, still busy on their codifying, to help secure a significant reduction in the indiscriminate incidence of the death penalty. A major part of the Second Report of the Commissioners was to deal with capital punishment.[10] In asking them to assist him on this burning issue of the day, the Home Secretary, who had carried the Reform Act and was now at the zenith of his popularity, was hoping to use their report to ensure the smooth passage through Parliament of his own proposed Bills to put an end to the gallows for most crimes.

A significant movement against the "Bloody Code", with death as the penalty for over 200 crimes (many of them minor), had been growing in the

---

7. *Parliamentary Papers.* (1836) Second Report of the Criminal Law Commissioners, "Defence of Prisoners by Counsel". vol. xxxvi.
8. *Hansard.* 3rd series, vol. 31, col. 1142.
9. 6 and 7 Will. IV. c. 114.
10. *Parliamentary Papers.* (1836) xxxvi. p. 183.

country for over half a century. This was fuelled largely by the middle=class and the main issues involved were the inhumanity of the sheer volume of capital statutes, the question of whether the death penalty was effective as a deterrent and necessary at all, and the effect of the uncertainty of punishment caused by the arbitrary selection of only a proportion of those convicted to be executed.

As we have seen, Beccaria pointed the way and it was from his brilliant indictment that the crusade against capital punishment gradually developed in England. Bentham too had campaigned against the death penalty and the Commissioners acknowledged their debt to both Beccaria and Bentham. As a prelude to the campaign, and before the Commissioners were appointed, Sir Robert Peel had removed the threat of death from a number of capital offences. But he had only partly fulfilled his promise to "break the sleep of centuries", with the "Bloody Code" still in force and the influence of Paley's ideology for hanging still potent in certain circles.

Yet public opinion was finally becoming ready to reject the Paleian doctrine and the scene was set for the onslaught on the death penalty of Lord John Russell with help from the Commissioners. In their Second Report the Commissioners described Beccaria's theories as "sound and conclusive principles of penal legislation" and they used them as a framework for their own views and proposals on punishment. Beccaria's work had taken longer to penetrate English penal thinking than on the continent but his day had finally arrived. In support of the Commissioners, the influential *Law Magazine* declared that the death penalty should be confined to the highest order of crimes, that transportation should cease, and that it was imperative that the whole system of secondary punishments be revised.[11]

The Commissioners strongly rejected Paley and all he stood for. They submitted his arguments to detailed examination and rejected them outright with strong reasoning. Whilst they were collecting evidence, the movement against the death penalty was growing ever more powerful and the country abounded with tracts and tables claiming to have been inspired by Beccaria. The Commissioners took evidence from a number of eminent lawyers and others employed in the criminal justice system and concluded that a

---

11. *Law Magazine*. (1836) vol. 16, pp. 375-6.

repeal of the number of offences which were capital would not result in an increase in crime.

Providing another justification for reform they suggested that a great alteration in opinions and manners had made the frequent infliction of capital punishment less acceptable than it might have been in former ages, when human life was cheaper and offenders were more violent. And they forecast that continued progress in social improvement would provide the necessary inducement for still further mitigation in the severity of criminal justice. They finally came to the conclusion that the punishment of death should be limited to crimes of special atrocity. This meant crimes of high treason and offences involving aggravated violence to the person or endangering human life.

Once the report was finished it was delivered to Lord Chancellor Cottenham on 9 June 1836.

Parliamentary Response

Lord John Russell then wrote to the Commissioners to inform them that, following their report the government would introduce a Bill on capital punishment in the House of Commons.[12] He wanted the Commissioners to consider what the principal heads of such a Bill should be. They responded immediately and submitted various draft Bills, the combined effect of which was to remove the punishment of death from more than three-quarters of the existing capital offences.

During the course of 1837, Russell, armed with the Commissioners' drafts, sponsored his own Bills in the House of Commons for the removal of the death penalty from 21 of the 37 offences still capital, and for restrictions in the use of such punishment for the remaining 16.[13] William Ewart proposed an amendment to remove capital punishment from all offences

---

12. *Parliamentary Papers.* (1837) xxxi, p.1.
13. *Hansard.* (1837) 3rd series, vol. 37, col. 709.

short of actual murder. Despite Lord Russell's opposition the amendment secured 72 votes against 73.[14]

Russell's Bills were enacted with great speed and soon the death penalty was actually inflicted only in cases of murder and treason. In the event, the contribution of the Commissioners proved to be of crucial assistance to the government in securing the abolition of capital punishment to this considerable extent. It was a fitting climax to the inspiration of Beccaria and Bentham and the work for reform of Romilly. It was also a substantial contribution to the rule of law which deplores harsh, cruel and unfair punishments.

Conclusion

So dependent on capital punishment had the criminal law been for centuries that this advance alone necessitated far-reaching changes in other areas of the law including secondary punishments to which the Commissioners also made a profound contribution. They failed to codify the criminal law,[15] which was the purpose for which they were appointed, but the reforms they secured, in addition to prisoners counsel and the death penalty, included more speedy trial of juveniles, giving increased powers to judges to vary punishments in some cases to prevent injustices, abolition of the pillory and forfeiture for high treason and felony, compensation for victims of fraud and many others. These reforms of the criminal law were an integral element in the powerful changes taking place in English society which had produced Adam Smith's *The Wealth of Nations,* Utilitarianism, classical liberalism and all that went with, and came from, the Reform Act 1832. They also added to the enlargement and strengthening of the impact of the concept of the rule of law to which the Commissioners were dedicated.

---

14. *Ibid.* col. 911.
15. For more on the Criminal Law Commissioners see John Hostettler. (1992) *The Politics of Criminal Law: Reform in the Nineteenth Century.* Chichester, Barry Rose Law Publishers.

Champions of the Rule of Law

CHAPTER 12

TERRORISM AND CIVIL LIBERTIES

Tony Blair: The Rule of Law versus Parliamentary Supremacy

Terrorism has, of course, a long history but it took on a new meaning with the horrendous bombings in New York and at the Pentagon on 11 September 2001. This was reinforced in England with the suicide attacks on underground trains and a bus in London on 7 July 2005. In response to these atrocities came a new threat to civil liberties, human rights and the rule of law. This was outlined in the speech of Prime Minster, Tony Blair, as soon as 5 August 2005, and referred to earlier in the *Introduction*, when he said that, "the rules of the game are changing". This was compounded in a serious article he wrote for the *Sunday Times* on 27 May 2007.

In this, he first complained of the government's new anti-terror laws having been struck down by the courts in December 2004. Lord Hoffman had said that there was a greater risk to Britain through the abrogation of the foreign suspects' civil liberties than through terrorism. But to Blair the argument that the right to traditional civil liberties comes first was both misguided and wrong and a dangerous misjudgement. Thus, in a few words, he dismissed the fruits of centuries of struggle in this country for human rights and the rule of law.

Earlier in the same year the government introduced control orders by which, under the Prevention of Terrorism Act 2005[1], the Home Secretary could place restrictions on people suspected of terrorism. As already noticed these restrictions can involve what in effect amounts to house arrest, they determine whom suspects can meet, and mean fitting them with an electronic tag. The penalty for a breach of any one or more of the conditions is a sentence of imprisonment for up to five years. Since they dispense with not only

---

1. C. 2.

with a fair trial but any trial at all at this stage, control orders came under under severe attack even within the Coalition government after, according to Blair, having being "constantly attacked on civil liberty grounds". In 2011 they were replaced by new powers although these remain controversial.

And apart from internment without trial there can be "trials" that are also suspect. Accordingly, in June 2009 a court consisting of nine law lords held that reliance on secret evidence in a case against unnamed defendants had denied them a fair trial under the Human Rights Act 1998. In an earlier case the House of Lords had already declared that an 18-hour curfew was also a breach of human rights.

The United States

The situation has been even worse in the United States of America. Within five weeks of 11 September 2001, the extremely lengthy Patriot Act[2], extending to 134 pages, was passed by both Houses of Congress with bi-partisan support but with hardly any debate, and signed into law by President George W. Bush on 26 October 2001. This Act contained widespread provisions to curtail civil liberties and dramatically expanded wide and sweeping search and surveillance powers to American law enforcement agencies. At the same time it eliminated the checks and balances that enable the courts to ensure that such powers are not abused. Under the Act the government can monitor an individual's internet records, use roving wiretaps to monitor phone calls and investigate United States' citizens who are exercising legitimate protests. The Act was intended to have a limited life but, in July 2005, it was re-authorised with minor changes and, as amended, passed into law in March 2006. The consequences for civil liberties and the rule of law have been severe with many innocent people detained without trial, losing the right to privacy and having their characters smeared.

---

2. Full title: Uniting and Strengthening America by Providing Appropriate Tools Required to Intercept and Obstruct Terrorism Act 2001 (USA Patriot Act)

Guantánamo Bay

Another response to terrorism was the setting up of the black hole detention camp at Guantánamo Bay located at the US Naval Base in Cuba. This has been in operation since 11 January 2002. It first consisted of three camps: Camp Delta, Camp Iguana and Camp X-Ray, the last of which is now closed. Being in Cuba the camp is considered to be outside United States legal jurisdiction and the Bush administration held that many hundreds of men detained there indefinitely without charge or trial were not entitled to any of the protection offered by the Geneva Conventions. That was until 29 June 2006 when, in the case of *Hamdan v. Rumsfeld,* the Supreme Court held that such detainees were entitled to *minimal* protection under Common Article 3 of the Geneva Conventions. It is believed that in all the United States had detained more than 80,000 people in various sites around the world.[3]

In 2008 in the case of *Boumediene v. Bush,* the Supreme Court further held that people detained had a right to *habeas corpus.* Justice Kennedy, in his judgment, cited *Magna Carta* and the *Case of the Five Knights* (mentioned in *Chapter 4* of this work) and declared that "The laws and Constitution are designed to survive, and remain in force in extraordinary times. Liberty and security" he said, thus refuting Tony Blair, "can be reconciled within the law".[4]

In fact, although it is justified in the name of national security, detention without trial weakens the framework of international human rights and facilitates the use of practices which have long been prohibited in international law. Many commentators and lawyers have alleged that acts amounting to severe torture have frequently been used against people who have not been charged or tried. Those held in Guantánamo Bay have, until recently, had no access to any court, legal counsel or family. There have been numerous suicide attempts arising from cruel, inhuman and degrading treatment.

As a consequence, on 22 January 2009 President Barak Obama suspended the proceedings of the Guantánamo military commission for 120 days and said the camps, and all other overseas detention centres would be closed

---

3. Intelligence and Security Committee Report on Rendition. (July 2007) Cm. 7171. paragraph 53.
4. 553 US (2008).

within twelve months. But, in May of that year the Senate blocked the funds needed to transfer or release prisoners held there causing the President to order the preparation of a Correctional Centre in Illinois to receive Guantánamo prisoners. This, however, was also opposed by Congress.

At the time of writing some detainees who were soldiers when arrested are now facing military justice in the camp following a ruling by the Supreme Court that the military commission system was unlawful. Others continue to be detained without charge or trial.

Waterboarding

Another form of torture is waterboarding. This consists of immobilising a person on his or her back with the head inclined downwards. Water is then poured over the face and forced into the lungs causing the prisoner to experience the sensations of choking to death and drowning. It has been reported that the Central Intelligence Agency was using waterboarding on prisoners and that the US Department of Justice has authorised the procedure. US government officials claimed that waterboarding was not a form of torture and were supported in this by George W Bush when he was President.

Yet, it causes panic, brain damage from oxygen deprivation, fear of death, lasting psychological damage and sometimes heart failure. It is, therefore, clearly torture, despite denials by US officials including former Vice-President Dick Cheney. It is clearly contrary to the United Nations Convention Against Torture which is absolute in its application and also the Universal Declaration of Human Rights which, by Article 5, prohibits torture, and cruel, inhuman and degrading treatment or punishment.

Waterboarding was officially brought to an end in the United States in January 2009 by President Obama, who conceded that it was a form of torture and a mistake. However, there is still some concern that it may continue to be used for training purposes.

Extraordinary Rendition

In law, rendition is the transfer of a person from one jurisdiction to another after relevant legal proceedings and according to law. Different considerations arise when a suspect is transferred from abroad for trial in Britain or the United States. In Britain, the House of Lords has decided that the courts should not try anyone brought into the country in breach of international law.[5] In the United States, however, if such a defendant is indicted in an American court the court will deal with the case in the normal manner.

Extraordinary rendition, however, is a similar transfer from one state to another but outside the law, i.e. illegally. It was described as "kidnapping" by Lord Steyn in his Attlee Foundation Lecture in April 2006

In practice, it is usually meant to connote the transfer of prisoners by the United States to countries known to torture suspects. It is widely believed, although denied by the USA government, that since 9 September 2001 some 3,000 people have been secretly transported by the US to countries around the world although this has been denied by administration officials. But according to a European Parliament report dated February 2007, the US Central intelligence Agency has conducted 1,245 flights, many of them to destinations where suspects could face torture. Despite Department of State denials of this, President Obama, within days of his Inauguration, signed an Executive Order opposing extraordinary rendition torture and setting-up a task force to recommend how to prevent it. The Bush administration admitted the practice but argued that they had asked the receiving countries not to use torture. Where a country habitually uses torture, however, it is hard to believe that it would refrain in such cases. It may be asked why else would the abduction take place?

However, in the United Kingdom the head of MI6, Sir John Sawers, has said that torture is abhorrent and rejected by his organization. British spies, he added, do not pass information on terrorist plots to foreign governments if there is a risk of suspects being tortured, even if it could prevent an attack. His agency would seek different means, compliant with human rights laws, to eliminate any threat. Some human rights groups, however, expressed scepticism.

---

5. *R. v. Horseferry Road Magistrates' Court, ex p. Bennett.* (1994) 1 AC. 42.

Champions of the Rule of Law

CHAPTER 13

SUMMING UP

Coke — "The Oracle of the Laws of England"

All the lawyers mentioned in this book have, in one way or another and in different historical situations, had a profound belief in, and effect upon, the rule of law and what it means in the lives of the people. They have helped refine a rule of law that is "highly sensitive to individual liberty and private property, and insistent upon the accountability of all action in the name of government".[1]

Sir Edward Coke, against considerable opposition, had to grapple with medieval law but still managed to oppose torture and excesses in the use of capital punishment. As Chief Justice his principled and unflinching conflict with the early Stuart kings destroyed both the right of the monarch to decide cases and to make law by Proclamations. At the same time he also severely restricted the royal prerogative. His large volumes of *Reports* together with his four *Institutes of the Laws of England* had a tremendous influence in firmly establishing the common law against the threat of the encroaching Roman-canon law from the continent of Europe. They also overcame the deadly influence of the outdated law of medieval times. And, they encouraged acceptance of the rule of law in its early stages.

Coke constantly urged the importance of *Magna Carta* as well as trial by jury and his giving strong support to the right to *habeas corpus* led him into the leadership of the libertarian group in Parliament. Here, he used his monumental knowledge of the law to encourage Members of Parliament to insist, against resistance from the king, not only upon their own privileges but upon the rights of the people. This led to his drafting the Petition of Right,

---

1. W.R. Cornish and G. De N. Clark. ((1989) *Law and Society in England 1750-1950*. London, Sweet & Maxwell, p. 12.

the first great constitutional document since *Magna Carta,* for the liberties of the people through the supremacy of the law and within the rule of law.

Matthew Hale

Sir Matthew Hale, apart from the one serious blemish in the witchcraft case (mentioned in *Chapter 3*), consistently endeavoured, particularly when a judge, to ensure that trials were fair and defendants treated civilly. His *Rules of Conduct* for himself and other judges exemplify the essence of the rule of law. Judges should not be rigid and should decline solicitations. To avoid bias with compassion to the poor or favour to the rich and reach no judgment until the whole case and both parties are heard. In criminal trials to incline to mercy and acquittal and to treat crimes that consist merely of words with moderation.

These were not precepts generally adopted by judges in Hale's day but they all point to a feeling for the rule of law and, in particular, for the need for a fair trial. And, like Coke, his written works on law, and his work on the Hale Commission, all added to the concept of the supremacy of law. His place in history survives because of his understanding and exposition of the crucial bedrock function of the rule of law in the flexible and changing constitution of this country.

Cesare Beccaria

The whole of Cesare Beccaria's book *On Crimes and Punishments* breathes the spirit of the rule of law. At a time when continental penal law was barbaric, accusations were secret, imprisonment was decided behind closed doors without trial and torture was endemic his *cri de coeur* echoed across Europe and his humanitarian proposals were adopted by one ruler after another. It even crossed to the new United States with the blessing of Thomas Jefferson. Beccaria pleaded for an end to torture and the gallows and for a complete reform of the law of punishments. This "counter-crime", as he described punishment, committed in the name of the law should be indulged in only to exclude some greater evil. The rule of law should be a binding force in a better kind of society based on humanity.

Beccaria was opposed to arbitrary rule, cruelty and to intolerance. He believed that criminal trials should be prompt and that punishments be fair and impartial. The reforms he proposed were meant to be part of a transformation to a more rational and enlightened society. And in a memorable sentence he summed up his message on penal law with the words: "In order that every punishment may not be an act of violence, committed by one man or by many against a single individual it ought to be above all things public, speedy, necessary, the least possible in the given circumstances, proportioned to its crime, dictated by the laws".

Thomas Jefferson

Jefferson is best known today as one of the founders of the United States and the author of the American Declaration of Independence. He is frequently referred to as one of the greatest of United States Presidents imbuing the new nation with democratic ideals. In a period of war he was Governor of the state of Virginia and, at different times, he was Minister to France, Secretary of State, Vice President and President. And underlying it all he was a lawyer who breathed the spirit of the rule of law.

Although an inspiring leader of the struggle for independence from Great Britain, he acknowledged the importance of the English common law, with its adversary trial, *habeas corpus* and trial by jury and fought bitterly, and successfully, to ensure that they were adopted in the new nation. Along with John Adams, another President, Jefferson transferred the spirit of Beccaria's *On Crimes and Punishments* to the United States having translated it from its original Italian. And, of the ten Amendments to the US Constitution, ratified in 1791 as the *Bill of Rights,* six are crucial elements of the rule of law.

With trial by jury Jefferson wished to go further than the law in England and have the jurors decide questions of law as well as questions of fact. He held that trial by jury was the only anchor man had devised by which a government could be restrained from abuse of power. He was the first to give expression to the principle that all men are created equal and have the inalienable rights to life, liberty and the pursuit of happiness. He also urged the state legislature of Virginia to abolish the death penalty for all crimes other than murder and treason and he spoke out for speedy trials, the right of defendants to call witnesses and have the assistance of counsel in his defence.

To Jefferson the rule of law was not only an essential cornerstone for the fabric of democratic society it was also truly ennobling. He was a staunch advocate of liberty and a great legislator, statesman and President.

Jeremy Bentham

Although Bentham said that the rule of law was a "nonsense on stilts" and that every law was an infraction of liberty he could not have meant those words to be taken literally as he endeavoured to secure definitive codes of law for countries across the globe. He was deeply influenced by Beccaria, as he openly acknowledged. In terms of the rule of law he argued, ahead of his time, that the death penalty should be abolished and that personal liberty should be protected.

In place of the gallows he proposed that imprisonment be improved and, at some cost in time and money, he put before Parliament a blueprint for a new kind of prison to be called a Panopticon. This was to be a circular iron and glass building where the Governor would be able to see each prisoner at all times without being seen by them and could direct them without leaving his post. "The spider in his web", commented Burke. Financial arrangements proposed by Bentham were meant to ensure that prisoners were paid for work thus replacing the unsatisfactory system whereby prisoners paid fees to their gaolers. Although Parliament agreed to this cyclopic monster in 1794, it was never built at the Millbank site purchased for it where the Tate Gallery now stands. One was built in America, however, and another in Breda in Holland where it still stands.

He opposed torture, except in one type of case and advocated that the law should be written in clear terms and free from ambiguity, obscurity and bulkiness and be made available to all. What he disliked were judges and the unwritten common law with its judicial law-making. But he knew there could be no society or government without law and he sought to rescue it from the obscurity and the oppressive function which he, correctly, attributed to it in his day. And, punishment, which was itself an evil, could be acceptable if it promised to exclude a greater evil than itself. As with Beccaria, he believed the vital object of punishment was to protect society and not to inflict torments on the offender.

Despite his protestations to the contrary, he spoke out for making the cruel and arbitrary criminal law more civilized and humane than it was and his works, particularly on punishments, adhere to the Beccarian principles of the rule of law. As a consequence, numerous reforms of the criminal law which he advocated, either by trenchant criticism of existing rules, or by positive proposals for new ones, have gradually been woven into the fabric of the law with substantially beneficial results. Much of the credit for this must also go to the more practical minds of Romilly, Peel, Brougham and the Criminal Law Commissioners who, following his example, helped bring our criminal law out of its dark medieval past into the modern world.

Thomas Erskine

Erskine was lauded by his contemporaries in the law for his spellbinding eloquence. Brougham described his voice as of surpassing sweetness, clear, flexible, strong, earnest and free from harshness or monotony. To which the *Edinburgh Review* added a description of "the witchery of this extraordinary man's voice, eye and action". But beyond these tributes is what he told juries in the defence of liberty and the rule of law.

In a period when the government of William Pitt took fright at the idea of the French Revolution spreading to Britain, his greatest triumph was in his defence of three prisoners in the infamous treason trials of 1794. Without his success in securing the rejection of 800 warrants for arrest of prominent citizens, the country would have descended into the darkness of prolonged oppression. The eminent historian, J R Green, described the government's excesses in the prosecutions and attacks on freedom at the time as the "English Terror".[2] In similar vein Lord John Campbell called the frenzied attempts

---

2. J.R. Green. (1874) *A Short History of the English People.* London, Folio Society edn. (1992), p.

at repression, "a Reign of Terror".³ In unprecedented scenes in court, where there was an open presumption of guilt, Erskine won over the jury and decisively turned these three trials against the government. In doing so he not only cut down the law of constructive treason but also helped preserve freedom and the rule of law in England.

In the case of the *House of Commons v. Stockdale*, with his "Indian Chief" speech, Erskine won a verdict which established the freedom of the press and in trial after trial on charges of treason and sedition he ensured a fair trial, and often victory, for the accused. He would relentlessly attack "unyielding injustice" and ask juries to uphold liberty. In the trial of John Frost he upheld the presumption of innocence and, comparing the common law with the "vexatious system of inquisition [that] began and ended with the Star Chamber", said that the common law's dignified and humane policy soared above the little irregularities of lives and disdained to "enter our closets without a warrant".

Erskine was one of the greatest forensic lawyers ever to appear in English criminal courts. His criminal cases may well be called "Trials of British Freedom" and he helped inspire human rights defence lawyers of today. To the benefit of us all he used his skills as an advocate at every opportunity to uphold liberty and the rule of law in a time of heavy handed repression.

Samuel Romilly

Romilly's great claim to fame comes from the greatest labour of his life, the efforts in the House of Commons, against pitiless opposition, to reform the cruel and arbitrary criminal law of England. It was the time of the "Bloody Code" under which committing one of over 200 crimes, many of them trivial, could lead a man to the hangman's noose. His early opposition to the fashionable, but deadly, theories of punishment of Martin Madan and William Paley led him to a mature theory of penal reform that he advocated throughout his life in Parliament.

818.
3. Lord John Campbell. (1847) *Lives of the Chancellors*. London, John Murray, vol. vi, p. 460.

He consistently endeavoured to get the Admiralty to end the flogging of seamen with a thousand or more lashes, even for minor offences, which often resulted in death. He intervened in the debate on a Bill to extend transportation and imprisonment in the hulks on the Thames, citing the cases of young children who were incarcerated in these living hells. His efforts to abolish the death penalty for minor crimes were unfailing although he only partially succeeded. At all stages he came up against the unfeeling opposition of senior judges, such as Lord Chancellor Eldon and Lord Chief Justice Ellenborough, and peers in the House of Lords who believed in severity rather than that the principal aim of punishment should be the reformation of the criminal.

Ultimately, he secured the enactment of six statutes to remove the death penalty for certain crimes and his speeches made a deep and lasting impression on public opinion and many MPs. Following his death, his followers continued the battle and eventually, in 1837, secured the removal of capital punishment from most offences so that before long it remained only for murder and treason. He had played a significant part in reducing the incidence of the death penalty and reforming the criminal law and his insistence on the rule of law was vindicated.

William Garrow

If the rule of law cannot exist without defendants having a fair trial, Sir William Garrow certainly played a crucial part in cementing that element of it. By his vigorous cross-examination of unscrupulous prosecutors and persistently insisting on criminal rules of evidence he played a crucial role in destroying the credibility of thief-takers and establishing adversary trial in England. This became England's gift to the world when adversariality was adopted in the United States and common law countries across the globe. Today, it is being adopted – albeit sometimes slowly – in fresh countries in Asia, Europe and South America.

Yet, Garrow's story has been kept from the general public by an intriguing quirk of history. But, with the BBC TV programme "Garrow's Law" and the biography *Sir William Garrow: His Life, Times and Fight for Justice*, he now has his place in the public-eye for his daring challenge to the entrenched legal establishment of his day. Apart from being the "father of adversary trial", he changed the dynamic of criminal trials by helping to secure the dominance of the presumption of innocence and many rules of evidence, such as the rule against hearsay, to assist prisoners in their defence. Although unwittingly, Garrow made a major contribution to enhancing and expanding the meaning of both the rule of law and human rights.

The Criminal Law Commissioners

The 1833 Criminal Law Commissioners were a Benthamite body of eminent lawyers who based their approach to penal law on the work of Beccaria. At the time, as W R Cornish has written:

> The long dispute over the death penalty lay near the very eye of political life. The eighteenth century ruling class – small in number, hungry for property and its attendant power – had to maintain stability and order without the civil police of modern times. Capital punishment formed an ugly apex to a system of social control through legal processes which functioned to a significant degree at the pleasure of the governors.[4]

Accordingly, they responded swiftly to the request of Lord John Russell, the Home Secretary, to assist him in reducing the incidence of the death penalty. They completely demolished the argument of William Paley for a greater use of judicial discretion in punishment. And they prepared a report which formed the basis of the Bills Russell introduced in the House of Commons and was used by Lord Lyndhurst to secure support in the House of Lords which had always stood in the way of such reform. As a consequence, the death penalty was removed from 21 of the 37 offences still capital and restricted its use in the 16 remaining. Shortly afterwards, as we have seen, the death penalty came to be inflicted only for the crimes of murder and treason.

---

4. W.R. Cornish. (1978) *Criminal Justice and Punishment*. In Cornish and others. *Crime and Law in Nineteenth Century Britain*. Dublin, Irish University Press, p. 18.

The Commissioners also produced another report which played a significant part in assisting Russell to secure the enactment of the Prisoners Counsel Act 1836 which finally completed the work of Garrow and secured the right of defendants to have counsel appear for their defence in all trials. In all their eight reports they extolled the rule of law and secured a more speedy trial for juvenile offenders who often languished in adult gaols to their detriment for many months. Their reports resulted in an increase in the powers of judges to vary punishments in some cases to avoid injustices and, *inter alia,* helped secure the abolition of the pillory and forfeiture for high treason and felony. In so doing they assisted in the reform of the harsh criminal law of their day and generally enhanced the meaning and scope of the rule of law.

Conclusion

In the past the rule of law always had a narrower meaning than it has today. But, in their own way, all the lawyers portrayed here did their best in the circumstances of the time to support it often with some personal sacrifice as with Coke who was imprisoned for his pains, and Beccaria who came under ferocious attack from the Roman Catholic Church, and had, initially, to publish his book anonymously. Erskine too was bitterly attacked and suffered dismissal as Attorney-General to the Prince of Wales for defending Tom Paine. All of them, without exception were ahead of their time and should be seen as enlightened heroes in the struggle for the rule of law and human rights which is still continuing today. They are an inspiration to those who wish to continue in their footsteps.

Champions of the Rule of Law

CHAPTER 14

AFTERWORD

Breaching the Rule of Law

As the title indicates this book deals with the approach to the rule of law of major English and United States lawyers. Insofar as in this *Afterword* I recall, as a solicitor, some trials in which I have been involved, it is on a far lower plane than the level of the legal eagles described in earlier chapters. In fact, more like the contribution of a sparrow in comparison. But my examples do reveal modern-day breaches of the rule of law which should remind us to be ever vigilant against such injustices. Except for the trial of the "Birmingham Six" in which I was not involved, I introduce them chronologically and not on the basis of their significance.

These cases, however, are not included merely to recount my own experiences but to illustrate that the rule of law is a live issue in countless everyday contexts of which they serve as examples. Readers will have other experiences. Some people want to take short cuts or keep things to themselves. Vigilance is needed to avoid thinking that lip-service to the rule is sufficient or that it should be over-ridden in the interests of security or expediency.

London

During the 1950s and 1960s, from my office in Covent Garden, I was involved in a number of civil liberty cases in which some defendants who were engaged in lawful protest on one issue or another that they believed important were arrested by police and charged with loitering with intent to steal or similar offences. It was a police practice that became known as "sus" i.e. allowing the police to act on suspicion alone. If a politically committed young person was chalking a slogan on a wall it was not difficult for a police officer to allege he was intending to steal from a nearby car! Although it is hard to imagine car thieves indulging in daubing on hoardings.

Others were charged with causing a breach of the peace at meetings when the prosecution showed no evidence that a breach of the peace had occurred or was even likely to occur. On occasion, the police used brutality but even photographs of this (in one case against a severely disabled person) produced no reaction of sympathy from magistrates who at that time appeared to believe police evidence was sacrosanct, as was later put into words by the late Lord Denning.

In 1975 the "Birmingham Six" were sentenced to life imprisonment for allegedly having committed murder and conspiring to cause explosions in Birmingham. On a subsequent appeal, Lord Denning said that if these six men were not guilty it would mean that the police were guilty of perjury, violence and threats and that the confessions they had made were involuntary and not properly admitted in evidence. That he said was an "appalling vista". Notwithstanding, on 14 March 1991 the Court of Appeal overturned the convictions on the ground that the police had both fabricated and suppressed evidence.

In my cases, in magistrates' courts and Quarter Sessions, which were far less dramatic, occasionally the defence were successful but often the defendants were left with a stain on their character, and sometimes suffered imprisonment, solely as a result of police "evidence". Each of them had their lives seriously affected. Nowadays the conduct of the police is much more circumscribed but miscarriages of justice still occur and must be strongly guarded against.

Belfast Murder Trial

In the past I have attended trials outside England as an observer in Germany and Nigeria. And, in August 1958, I travelled to Belfast as observer for the Connolly Association at the trial, before Mr Justice Black and a jury at the Belfast City Commission, of Kevin Mallon and Francis Patrick Talbot. They were two 21-year-old youths who were charged with murdering a police sergeant with a booby-trap bomb. This was, of course, well before the

"Birmingham Six" trial. F Elwyn Jones QC (later Lord Chancellor) appeared for the defence. The trial lasted just over a week and the accused were alleged to have confessed to the murder. However, the defence submitted that the "confessions" should not be put in evidence before the jury on two grounds:

> that they were secured while the accused were in illegal custody; and
> that they were induced by "undue terror and menaces".

I met the two youths in the cells under the courthouse and they told me they had indeed been ill-treated with one police questioner "behaving like a maniac". Sisters of the accused, Sheila Mallon and Kathleen Talbot, gave evidence that when they had visited their brothers in prison they had witnessed marks of beatings on their bodies. Kathleen Talbot testified that when she saw her brother in prison three weeks after his arrest his face "looked horrible, his eyes were sunk and his lips swollen". However, believing, as Lord Denning did later that the police who denied the beatings would not commit perjury, the judge rejected both submissions.

During the lengthy trial it was clear that the evidence against the accused was circumstantial. They gave their testimony clearly and both stood up well to cross-examination by the Attorney-General and his experienced colleagues. After a week of evidence the jury took two and a quarter hours to consider their verdict and when they returned to the court the foreman announced that they found both the defendants "not guilty". The Attorney-General told the judge there were no further charges but, after being allowed to see their families for half an hour, both defendants were re-arrested in the court and returned to prison without charge.

Here was clearly a breach of the rule of law as was the rejection of the defence plea on the "confessions".

Arms Factory Raid

My attendance at the Mallon and Talbot trial and the booklet I wrote about it may have led to my receiving instructions to act for Patrick O'Sullivan, a young man from County Cork who belonged to the Irish Republican

Army (IRA), and Connor Lynch who was a member of Sinn Fein. They were charged at the Old Bailey with raiding an arms factory and assaulting a watchman in Dagenham, to the east of London. Each pleaded not guilty and I briefed the well-known civil rights barrister, John Platts Mills, to defend them. The prosecution placed in court in full view of the jury a large number of machine guns and ammunition. This was despite the fact that no weapons had been stolen because the watchman had set his Alsatian dog on the alleged thieves who had run away empty-handed. In any event, the defendants should have been presumed innocent unless, or until, proved guilty. Platts Mills asked that the weapons and ammunition be removed since their presence in court was clearly prejudicial to a fair trial for his clients. This was refused by the judge and both men were later found guilty and sentenced to seven years in prison. Again, a breach of the rule of law in that defendant's should have a trial that is not only fair but seen to be fair.

Flogging in Aden

In mid-November 1962 I was asked by the Aden Trades Union Congress to apply to the High Court in Aden for bail for their leader Abdul al-Asnag who was being held in prison awaiting trial for alleged sedition. At the time Aden, a British colony, was about to be forcibly merged with the nearby backward sheikdoms of the Federation of South Arabia, a process to which the Aden TUC was opposed. The authorities clearly considered it wise to have Asnag, and other leaders who had led demonstrations against the merger, behind bars. Accordingly I flew to Aden where I obtained permission, as a solicitor, to act in effect as a barrister to enable me to appear in court. In sweltering heat the courtroom resembled a bear garden, as in William Garrow's day, until the time came for the judge to preside over the session when order was restored.

After the hearing, in which bail was refused, I visited Asnag in prison to discuss a possible appeal where I also had an interview with the prison superintendent in his room overlooking the prison yard, about 20 yards away. At one point he was telephoned and left the room apologising and saying he would return shortly. Looking through the picture window into

Afterword

the yard I saw a pre-fabricated scaffolding being erected and then five out of an intended eleven Arabic Aden TUC members were brought out and flogged. The flogging was barbaric. The men were stripped and their hands and feet were tied face down to the rack with muslin covering their buttocks. Each received twelve strokes and their screaming made my stomach turn. Sickened, I left the prison without awaiting the return of the superintendent. The accompanying photograph (here shown for the first time in the UK) reveals the effects of the flogging which can only be considered to be torture.

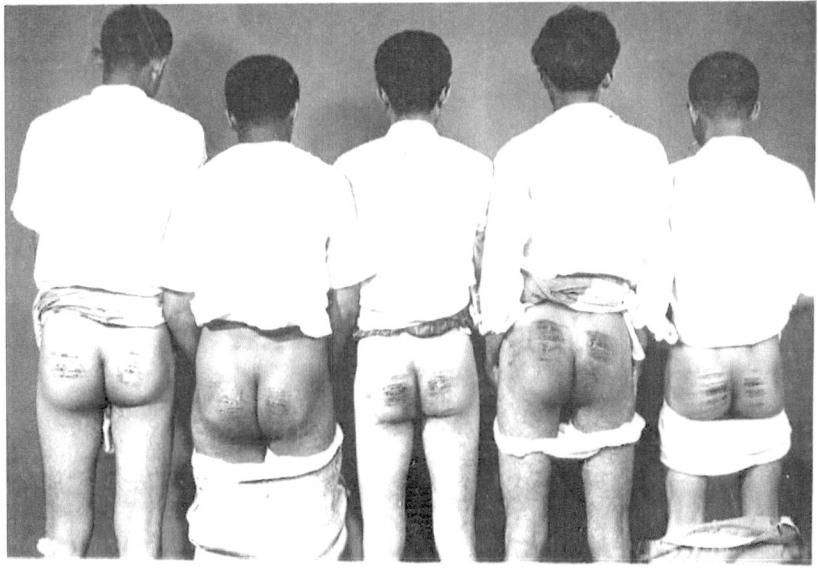

Original photograph in the possession of the author

I was told later that the men were flogged for planning a hunger strike in sympathy with a prisoner who had been put in solitary confinement for not allowing the prison dentist to take out an aching tooth when he was due for release the next day.

Later that evening the Aden Attorney-General asked me to keep quiet about the incident. But it was too late. When I had left the prison a member of Reuters news agency approached me in the street and asked me what had happened inside. I told him. That was immediately relayed to newspapers in

London and elsewhere in the world. Unknown to me the House of Commons at Westminster was debating the situation in Aden for the first time in its history.

When I returned to London Airport (as Heathrow was then called) I was approached by an MP's secretary who took me to the House of Commons, where, in a committee room, I outlined what I had seen to a number of MPs. This was reported to the House by Robert Edwards, MP for Bilston, who said he found it difficult to participate in the debate without some emotion. He told Members what I had seen and added that he knew these Arab trade union leaders and knew them to be "cultured men, clerks, technical assistants, school teachers and scientists and this was a terrible indignity committed against them".[1] The next day most of the media reported the facts and condemned the floggings editorially. I understand the report by Robert Edwards in Parliament also had a considerable effect in the Middle East.

Whilst I was in Aden the British Governor and Commander-in-Chief was Sir Charles Johnston who, on his return to Britain, wrote a book entitled, *The View from Steamer Point: Three crucial years in South Arabia*. At the time Steamer Point was a tourist area of the colony which was built on an extinct volcano that gave its name to the area known as Crater. In the book (on page 131) he refers to my visit and to the floggings as "canings" and says "this measure of prison discipline produced an 'emotional effect' in the British press when described in the House of Commons debate". He also wrote that the prison superintendent, a "senior Adenese official of Arab-Somali extraction", feared a riot and people who criticised corporal punishment in this context were "coddling their own consciences at the expense of reality".

Fortunately, the British government took a more realistic view of the incident than its Aden Governor. As a consequence, I was invited to meet Mr Duncan Sandys, Winston Churchill's son-in-law and Secretary of State for Commonwealth Relations as well as Secretary of State for the Colonies. However, he had to go abroad at the appointed time. Accordingly, I was seen by the Colonial Under-Secretary, Mr Nigel Fisher, in his office, a beautiful large room with two dogs settled on the carpet in front of the fireplace. I repeated what I had seen and he told me he was taking the situation very

---

1. *Hansard.* (13 November 1962) vol. 667, no. 11, cols. 307-308.

seriously. As, indeed, he did, for soon afterwards it was announced in the House of Lords that, except in cases of mutiny, flogging was to be abolished in all British colonial prisons.

It seems that it was not only in Aden that such cruelty could be used and it is noteworthy that it was only by my chance meeting in the superintendent's office at a particular moment that this serious breach of the rule of law was discovered. Again it reflects the overriding need for transparency in government and its close attachment to the rule of law in its dealings abroad as well as at home.

Champions of the Rule of Law

SELECT BIBLIOGRAPHY

Primary Sources

Amos, Andrew. (1856) *The Ruins of Time exemplified in Sir Matthew Hale's History of the Pleas of the Crown.* London, V. & R. Stevens & G.S. Norton.
Aristotle. *Politics.* (1923) Oxford, The Clarendon Press.
Austin, John. (1861) *The Province of Jurisprudence Determined.* (1955 edition), Cambridge, Cambridge University Press.
Beccaria, Cesare. (1775) *An Essay on Crimes and Punishments with a Commentary Attributed to Monsieur De Voltaire.* 4th edn. London, F. Newbery.
Bentham, Jeremy. (1827) *Rationale of Judicial Evidence, Specially Applied to English Practice.* London, Hunt and Clarke.
Bracton, Henry de. (c. 1250) *De Legibus Tractabus Consuetudinibus* (Treatise on the Laws and Customs of England).
Brougham, Henry, Lord. (1838) *Speeches.* Edinburgh, Adam and Charles Black
 (1839) *Historical Sketches of Statesmen who Flourished in the Time of George III.* London, Charles Knight & Co.
Burnett, Bishop Gilbert. (1856) *The Life and Death of Sir Matthew Hale.* Oxford, Oxford University Press.
Campbell, Lord John. (1847) *Lives of the Chancellors.* London, John Murray.
 (1849) *Lives of the Chief Justices of England.* London, John Murray.
Cobbett, William. (1809-1828) *State Trials.* London, R. Bagshaw.
Coke, Sir Edward. (1600-1642) *Reports.*
 (1823 edn.) *1 Institute – Littleton* (with notes by Francis Hargrave and Charles Butler and Hale (LCJ) and Nottingham (LCJ).
 (1797) *2-4 Institutes of the Laws of England.* London, E. & R. Brooke.
Fortescue, John. (1470) *Tractatus de Laudibus.*
Foster, Sir Michael. (1762) *A Report of some Proceedings on the Commission of Oyez and Terminer and Gaol Delivery for the Trial of the Rebels in 1746 and other Crown Cases.* Oxford, Clarendon Press.
Hale, Sir Matthew. (1736) *The History of the Pleas of the Crown.* London, E. And R. Nutt and R. Gosling.

Howell's *State Trials.* (1789)
Hardwicke Papers. (1652) British Library, *Add. MSS.* 35863.
Madan, Martin. (1785) *Thoughts on Executive Justice.* London, J. Dodsley.
Old Bailey Proceedings. (www.oldbaileyonline.org)
Paley, William. (1786) *Principles of Moral and Political Philosophy.* London, T. & J. Allman.
Parliamentary History. (1626), (1628), (1795), (1836), (1837).
Parliamentary Papers. (1836) Second Report of the Criminal Law Commissioners. "Defence of Prisoners by Counsel".
Polson, Archer. (1841) *Law and Lawyers, or Sketches and Illustrations of Legal History and Biography.* 2 vols. Philadelphia, Carey & Hart.
Romilly, Samuel. (1786) *Observations on a late Publication intituled Thoughts on Executive Justice.* London.
  (1820) *Speeches in the House of Commons.* London.
  (1840) *Memoirs of the Life of Sir Samuel Romilly Written by Himself and Edited by his Sons.* London, John Murray.
Year Books. 30 and 31, Edw. I. (Rolls Series).

Journals and Newspapers

Edinburgh Review. (1810), (1811-12), (1837), 1838).
Gentlemen's Magazine. (1836), (1851).
Journals of the House of Commons. (1652)
Law Magazine. (1836)
Hansard. (1836), (1837)
The Times. (1834)

Books and Articles

Adams, Charles Francis. (1856) *The Works of John Adams, second President of the United States with a life of the author, notes and illustrations.* Boston, Little Brown.
Baker, J.H. (1979) *An Introduction to Legal History.* London, Butterworths.

Select Bibliography

Beattie, J.M. (1991) "Garrow for the Defence". *History Today*. History Today Ltd.
  (1991) "Scales of Justice: Defence Counsel and the English Criminal Trial in the Eighteenth and Nineteenth Centuries". 9(2) *Law and History Review*. University of Illinois Press.
Bingham, Tom. (2010) *The Rule of Law*. London, Allen Lane.
Birks. T.R. (1874) Modern Utilitarianism. London, Macmillan & Co.
Bowen, Catherine Drinker. (1957) *The Lion and the Throne: The Life and Times of Sir Edward Coke*. London, Hamish Hamilton.
Carr, Sir Cecil. (1955) *A Victorian Law Reformer's Correspondence*. London, Quaritch.
Churchill, Winston. (1957) *A History of the English-Speaking Peoples*. London, Cassell & Co.
Cooke, Alistair. (1973) *America*. London, British Broadcasting Corporation.
Cotterell, Mary. (1968) "Interregnum Law Reform: The Hale Commission of 1652". *English Historical Review*.
Cornish, W.R. (1978) "Criminal Justice and Punishment". In Cornish and others. *Crime and Law in Nineteenth Century Britain*. Dublin, Irish University Press.
  with Clark, G. de N. (1989) *Law and Society in England 1750-1950*. London, Sweet & Maxwell.
Cromartie, Alan. (1995) *Sir Matthew Hale 1609-1676: Law, religion and natural philosophy*. Cambridge, Cambridge University Press.
Dicey, A.V. (1950 edn.) *Introduction to the Study of the Law of the Constitution*. London, Macmillan & Co. Ltd.
Farrer, J.A. (1880) *Crimes and Punishments including a new translation of Beccaria's Dei Delitti e Delle Pene*. London, Chatto & Windus.
Gardiner, S.R. (1883) *History of England from the Accession of James I to the Outbreak of the Civil War 1603-1642*. London, Longmans, Green.
  (1906) *Constitutional Documents*. Oxford, Clarendon Press.
Grayling, A.C. (2007) *Towards the Light: the Story of the Struggles for Liberty and the Rights that made the Modern West*. London, Bloomsbury.
Hart, H.L.A. (1982) *Essays on Bentham: Studies in Jurisprudence and Political Theory*. Oxford, Clarendon Press.
Holdsworth, Sir William. (1966 edn,) *A History of English Law*. London, Methuen & Co. and Sweet and Maxwell.

(1966) *Some Makers of English Law.* Cambridge, Cambridge University Press.

Hostettler, John. (1997) *Sir Edward Coke: A Force for Freedom.* Chichester, Barry Rose Law Publishers.

(2002) *The Red Gown: The Life and Works of Sir Matthew Hale.* Chichester, Barry Rose Law Publishers.

(June 2004) "The Rule of Law v. Parliamentary Supremacy". Milton Keynes, *The Legal Executive Journal.*

(2004) *The Criminal Jury Old and New: Jury Power from Early Times to the Present Day.* Winchester, Waterside Press.

(2006) *Fighting for Justice: The History and Origins of Adversary Trial.* Winchester, Waterside Press.

(2010) With Richard Braby. *Sir William Garrow: His Life, Times and Fight for Justice.* Hook, Hampshire, Waterside Press.

(2010 reprint) *Thomas Erskine and Trial by Jury.* Hook Hampshire, Waterside Press.

(2010) *Cesare Beccaria: The Genius of 'On Crimes and Punishments'.* Hook, Hampshire, Waterside Press.

Jacobs, Sir Francis. (2007) *The Sovereignty of Law: The European Way.* Cambridge, Cambridge University Press.

Jardine, David. (1836) *A Reading on the Use of Torture in the Criminal Law of England Prior to the Commonwealth.* Given at New Inn Hall, Michaelmas Term *Edinburgh Review.* (April-July 1838).

Kidder, Frederic. (1870) *History of the Boston Massacre.* Albany, New York.

Landsman, S. (1983) "A Brief Survey of the Development of the Adversary System". 44(1) *Ohio State Law Journal.*

Langbein, John H. (2003) *The Origins of Adversary Criminal Trial.* Oxford, Oxford University Press

Lemmings, D. (2000) *Professors of the Law: Barristers and English Legal Culture in the Eighteenth Century.* Oxford, Oxford University Press.

Macaulay, Thomas Babington. (1980 edn.) *A History of England in the Eighteenth Century.* London, Folio Society.

Maestro, Marcello. (1973) *Cesare Beccaria and the Origins of Penal Reform.* Philadelphia, Temple University Press.

Marsh, Henry. (1971) *Documents of Liberty from earliest times to universal suffrage.* Newton Abbot, David and Charles (Publishers) Limited.

May, Allyson N. (2003) *The Bar and the Old Bailey, 1750-1850*. Chapel Hill and London, The University of North Carolina Press.

Peterson, Merrill D. (1970) *Thomas Jefferson & the New Nation: A Biography*. New York, Oxford University Press.

Pollock & Maitland. 1968 edn.) *A History of English Law Before the Time of Edward I*. Cambridge, Cambridge University Press.

Prall, Stuart E. (1966) *The Agitation for Law Reform during the Puritan Revolution, 1640-1660*.

Radzinowicz, Leon. (1948) *A History of English Criminal Law and its Administration from 1750. The Movement for Reform*. London, Stevens & Sons.

Rigg, James McMullen. (1975) *Dictionary of National Biography*.

Roscoe, Henry. (1833) *Lives of Eminent British Lawyers*. London, Longman, Rees, Orme, Brown, Green & Longman with John Taylor.

Stephen, James Fitzjames. (1883) *A History of the Criminal Law of England*. London, Macmillan.

Tamanaha, Brian Z. (2004) *On the Rule of Law*. Cambridge, Cambridge University Press.

Thompson, E.P. (1975) *Whigs and Hunters: The Origin of the Black Act*. London, Allen Lane.

Twining, Professor. (1973) "Bentham on Torture". *Northern Ireland Legal Quarterly*.

Vogler, Richard. (2005) *A World View of Criminal Justice*. Aldershot, Ashgate Publishing Limited.

(2006) *Criminal Justice and Due Process: A global Revolution?* Unpublished Lecture in Lewes, Sussex.

Williams, Sir John Bickerton. (1835) *The Memoirs of the Life, Character and Writings of Sir Matthew Hale*. London.

Champions of the Rule of Law

INDEX

7/7 *xvi, 22, 151*
9/11 *xv, 22, 151, 155*

A

Abinger, Lord Chief Baron *106*
abuse *96*
accomplices *137*
accountability *xii, 157*
accusation *89*
Act of Parliament *22, 45, 67*
Adams, John *64, 78*
Adams, John Quincey *79*
Aden *170*
administration of justice *21, 52*
administrative law *xi*
adversariality *64, 67, 73, 85, 97, 132, 136, 139, 140*
   Anglo-American adversary system of trial *139*
   origins of adversary trial *133*
advocates *99*
ambiguity *92*
American War of Independence *85, 86, 92, 102*
Amos, Andrew *60, 142*
Anglo-Saxon *84*
   Anglo-Saxon dooms *68*
   Anglo-Saxon times *63*
"appalling vista" *168*
Apprentices' Case, The *57*
arbitrariness *68, 75, 80, 98, 147*

arbitrary rule *32, 39*
Archbishop Laud *34*
Archbishop of Canterbury *128*
aristocracy *122*
Aristotle *20*
arms factory raid *169*
arrest *66, 74*
Assizes *122, 126, 136*
asylum *21*
   asylum seekers *xi*
Attorney-General *30, 34, 40, 44, 64, 69, 99, 108, 169*
   Attorney-General to the Prince of Wales *102*
autocracy *40*

B

bail *70*
   excessive bail *89*
barbarity *94*
barristers *131, 136, 138, 139, 144, 145*
   old Bailey hacks *131*
Bastille *74*
Beattie, John *132*
Beccaria, Cesare *xiv, 71, 86, 91, 117, 121, 122, 145, 147, 158*
Belfast murder trial *168*
benefit of clergy *61, 137*
Bentham, Jeremy *xiv, 61, 80, 87, 91, 117, 145, 147, 160*
beyond reasonable doubt *26*
bias *56, 89, 158*
biblical fundamentalism *56*

billetting *70*
Bill for Proportioning Crimes and Punishments in Cases heretofore Capital *86*
Billingsgate Boy *131*
Bill of Rights
   USA *xiv, 66, 80, 87, 138*
Bingham, Lord *20, 54*
Birmingham Six *167, 168*
biting off the ears *87*
Blackstone, William *29, 68, 123, 132*
Blair, Tony *22, 25, 81, 151, 153*
blood money *136*
Bloody Code *76, 119, 146, 162*
Bonham's Case *22, 67*
Boston Massacre *78*
Boumediene v. Bush *153*
bounty-hunters *136*
Bracton, Henry *xiii, 29, 37, 41, 69*
Bradshaw, John *48*
breach of the peace *168*
breaking on the wheel *71*
bribery *54*
   bribery in elections *111*
Brougham, Henry *60, 91, 92, 97, 106, 107, 112, 117, 126, 142, 145*
brutality *168*
bullying *59*
Burke, Edmund *99*
burning alive *128*
Bush, George W *81, 152, 154*
Buxton, Fowell *130*

C

"cab-rank" rule *109*
Campbell, Lord *67, 104*
Case of Proclamations *38, 42*
Catholics *30*
cause *69*
Central Intelligence Agency *154, 155*
certainty *xii, 126*
Chancery *66*
character smearing *152*
Charles I *33, 47, 48, 64, 68*
Charles II *52, 61*
Cheney, Dick *154*
Churchill, Winston *111*
civil
   civil death *70*
   civility *158*
   civil liberties *72, 81, 151, 152, 167*
   civil offences *37*
   civil society *xi*
   civil war *47*
class-bound procedures *27*
Coalition *25*
Code Louis *74*
codification
   Code Louis *74*
   Code of Conduct of the English Bar *109*
   criminal law code *61, 144*
   Napoleonic Code *74*
   penal code (France, etc.) *71*
   unalterable code *61*
Coercive Acts *84*

Coke, Edward *xiii, 22, 30, 52, 60, 63, 65, 84, 134, 145, 157*
Combination Laws *141*
common law *22, 29, 32, 41, 42, 61, 64, 66, 84, 89, 108, 139, 157*
  common law courts *51*
  unwritten common law *92*
Common Pleas *31, 38, 51, 69, 108*
Commonwealth *48*
compassing (imagining) the death of the King *57, 99*
compassion *53, 158*
compensation *88, 149*
confessions *33, 71, 76, 135, 137, 169*
conflict *139*
Connolly Association *168*
constitution *xi, 20, 23, 48, 65, 84, 89, 128*
  Constitutional Reform Act 2005 *xv, 21, 24, 25*
contempt *37*
contradictions *127*
control orders *20, 25, 151, 152*
Convention for the Protection of Human Rights and Fundamental Freedoms *138*
Cornish, W R *164*
corporal punishment *125, 170*
corresponding societies *111*
corruption *110, 111*
counsel *134*
  defence counsel *146*
  no-counsel rule *131, 134*
Court of Appeal *168*
Court of Chancery *32*
crime prevention *75, 87, 121, 122*

crimes consisting merely of words *158*
Criminal Evidence Act, 1898 *137*
criminal justice system *147*
criminal law *127*
Criminal Law Commissioners *xv, 60, 80, 97, 129, 161, 164*
Criminal Law Consolidation Acts of 1861 *143*
Cromwell, Oliver *42, 47*
cross-examination *135, 137, 139, 169*
Crown *29, 41, 47, 70*
cruelty *72, 80, 97, 159*
  cruel and unusual punishments *89*
  cruel, inhuman and degrading treatment *153, 154*
curfew *152*

D

death penalty *27, 35, 50, 54, 56, 60, 71, 76, 80, 86, 88, 93, 119, 123, 126, 130, 136, 141, 146*
declaration
  Declaration of Rights for Virginia *85*
  Declaration of the Rights of Man *xiv, 74*
defects *127*
defence *73*
De Laudibus *123*
democracy *19, 23, 36, 47, 107, 141*
  liberal democracy *xi*
Denning, Lord *168, 169*
depravity *127*
Desborough, Major-General *49*

183

detention *68*
  detention without charge *154*
  detention without trial *152, 153*
deterrence *35, 77, 97, 121, 147*
Dicey, A V *xv, 23, 24, 38, 138*
Dingler, George *135*
discretion *98, 126, 135*
  judicial discretion *122*
disembowelling *128*
disfiguring *87*
disorder *112*
dissent *125*
divine
  divine justice *53*
  divine right *41*
domestic law *xi*
double jeopardy *88*
due process *23, 64, 66, 88, 137*
dungeons *34*

E

Earl of Essex *30*
ecclesiastical law *37*
Edwards, Robert *172*
Eldon, John *100, 128*
electronic tagging *151*
Eliot, John *42*
Elizabeth I *34, 64*
Ellenborough, Lord *124, 128*
enlightenment *73, 74*
Enlightenment, The *97, 117*
equality *xi, 64, 67, 85, 94, 97*
  Equality and no King *108*

equality before the law *23*
equity *32*
Erskine, Thomas *xiv, 99, 161*
Europe *26, 29, 59, 71, 73, 138*
  medieval Europe *33*
European Convention on Human Rights
    xi, 22, 26, 27
evidence
  rules of evidence *135, 136, 139, 140*
Ewart, William *145, 148*
example *57*
excessive fines *89*
expediency *25, 91*
exploitation *107*
ex post facto legislation *98*
extraordinary rendition *21, 96, 155*
Eyre, Lord Chief Justice *99*

F

fairness *52, 64, 67, 158*
fair trial *19, 24, 25, 27, 138, 146, 163, 170*
false accusations *76*
Fawkes, Guy *34*
fear *121, 122, 123, 154*
felony *50, 57, 58, 123, 128, 134, 137, 145*
Felton's Case *34*
feudal relics *142*
fiction
  legal fiction *38*
Fisher, Nigel *172*
Five Knights' Case *69, 153*
floating prison *97, 127*
flogging *125, 163, 170*

184

forfeiture *149*
Fortescue *123*
Fox, Charles James *126*
Franklin, Benjamin *22*
fraud *149*
freedom *26, 30, 39, 67, 70, 71, 74, 100, 102, 110, 113*
  freedom of speech *39, 44*
  freedom of the press *102*
French Revolution *72, 92, 99, 108, 110, 128, 141, 161*
Frost, John *107, 162*
Fuller, Lon L. *26*

G

Garrow, William *xiv, 24, 75, 100, 112, 131, 145, 163*
  'Garrow's Law' *136*
Geneva Conventions *153*
Glorious Revolution *137, 142*
Gordon, Lord George *99*
Gordon Riots *118*
gouging out eyes *87*
greater evil *97*
Green, J R *161*
Guantánamo Bay *xv, 96, 153*

H

habeas corpus *24, 37, 63, 66, 68, 70, 72, 99, 111, 125, 153, 157, 159*
  Habeas Corpus Act 1679 *xiv, 69*

Habeas Corpus Suspension Act *113*
Hale Commission *48, 61, 158*
Hale, Matthew *xiii, 47, 51, 85, 145, 158*
Hamdan v. Rumsfeld *153*
happiness *85, 87, 91, 92, 123*
Hardy, Thomas *111, 112*
Hastings, Warren *103*
hearing both sides *38, 158*
hearsay *135, 137*
Heath, Robert *69*
Henry III *29*
High Court *68*
Hoffman, Lord *20, 25, 151*
Holdsworth, William *49, 62, 132*
Home Office *xi, 21*
Home Secretary *xi, 21, 130, 145, 146, 151*
Horne Tooke, John *111, 112*
house arrest *151*
House of Commons *39, 41, 44, 50, 102, 108, 112, 113, 125, 126, 148, 172*
  House of Commons v. Stockdale *102*
House of Lords *xi, 20, 49, 67, 70, 103, 120, 124, 126, 145, 155, 173*
Huguenot refugees *118*
hulks *97, 127*
humanitarianism *50, 117, 145*
humanity *33, 74, 124*
human rights *26, 64, 71, 73, 88, 138, 140, 151, 153*
  Human Rights Act 1998 *xv, 22, 27, 138, 152*
  Universal Declaration of Human Rights *154*
hunger strike *171*

I

ignorance of the law *xii*
Illinois Correctional Centre *154*
ill-treatment *169*
immunity from prosecution *137*
impartiality *62, 64, 159*
impeachment *103*
imprisonment *119, 121, 127, 160*
　imprisonment without trial *70*
Industrial Revolution *142*
informers *125*
inhumanity *73, 107, 147*
inhuman or degrading treatment *27*
innocence *75, 76*
Inns of Court *49*
inquisition *29*
inquisitorial system *71, 138*
insects in amber *60*
insurrection *99*
integrity *131*
international law *xi, 155*
intolerance *80, 159*
Irish Republican Army (IRA) *169*

J

Jacobites *111*
Jefferson, Thomas *xiv, 41, 64, 74, 78, 80, 83, 138, 159*
Jeffreys, Lord Chief Justice *134*
Johnston, Sir Charles *172*
Jones, F Elwyn *169*
judges *51, 92*

　acting as prosecutors *72*
　gifts to *54*
　independent *61*
judicial
　judicial caprice *87*
　judicial ethics *51*
　judicial ferocity *72*
　judicial independence *21*
　judicial law-making *92, 160*
　judicial review *21, 67*
judiciary *21, 22, 67, 72*
jurisdiction *153, 155*
jury *26, 29, 85, 112, 119, 138*
　grand juries *127*
　jury packing *61*
　jury trial *xiii*
　role of judge and jury *89*
　trial by jury *24, 35, 59, 65, 89, 157*
　trial by peers *36*
justice *107, 122*
　justice should be swift, etc. *87*
　lottery of justice *124*
　selling, denying, etc. *68*
justices of the peace *36, 127, 141*
just laws *xi*

K

Kafka, Franz *xii*
Kelyng, John *55, 57*
Kennedy, Justice (USA) *153*
Kenyon, Lord Chief Justice *109*
Ker, Henry Bellenden *142*
kidnapping *155*

King Charles I *xiii*
King James I *36, 40, 41*
King John *63, 65*
King's Bench *38, 69*
King William IV *142*

L

Landsman, Stephen *138*
Langbein, John H *133*
law *57*
  bad laws *27*
  bulkiness *92*
  clear and precise *75*
  clearly expressed *26*
  codification of the law *60, 93*
  demystifying the law *98*
  flexibility *122*
  fundamental law *69*
  impossiblility and *26*
  judicial law-making *98*
  law and fact *89*
  Law Lords *21*
  Law Magazine *147*
  law of the land *65*
  law reform *48*
  not contradictory *26*
  Of the Laws and Customs of England *29*
  penal law *91, 122*
  publication of *26*
  "rapid vegetation" of *61*
  retrospective laws bad *26*
  rule-bound law *124*
  science of law *92*
  supremacy of the law *158*
  tenderness of the law *124*
lawyers *49, 59, 78, 83, 91, 99, 114, 131, 145, 147, 153, 157, 167*
  assistance of counsel, etc. *89*
  duty to a client *48*
legal
  legal aid *51*
  legal argument *137*
  legal representation *27*
legislature *22*
legitimacy *51, 122, 141*
leniency *94*
lèse majesté *134*
lettres de cachet *72, 75*
liberalism
  classical liberalism *149*
liberty *39, 40, 65, 67, 68, 69, 74, 84, 88, 99, 106, 113, 157*
  every law an infraction of liberty *92*
  liberty of the press *103*
Liberty *25*
loitering with intent *167*
Long Parliament *45, 51*
Lord Chancellor *21, 25, 37, 100, 113, 142, 148*
Lynch, Connor *170*

M

Macaulay *111*
Mackintosh, James *130*
Madan, Reverend Martin *120, 122, 126*
magistrates' courts *168*

Magna Carta *xiii, 36, 40, 41, 43, 44, 63, 68, 153, 157, 158*
maiming *87*
Mallon, Kevin *168*
martial law *41, 45*
medieval law *157*
mercy *53, 87, 128, 137, 158*
Messenger's Case 57, 59
MI6 *155*
Midland Circuit *119*
military justice *154*
Millbank *160*
Mill, John Stuart *119*
minimum standards *25*
miscarriages of justice *61, 168*
mitigation *145*
moderation *53*
morality *26, 77, 92, 97*
  institutional morality *xi*
motive *97, 106*
murder *86*
mutiny *173*

N

Napoleonic Code *74*
Napoleonic Wars *141*
necklace *33*
nonsense on stilts *92*

O

oath *134*

defence witnesses *50*
ex officio oath *37*
judicial oath *31*
Oath of Supremacy *44*
prisoners able to take *137*
Obama, Barak *153, 155*
obscurity *92*
Old Bailey *xiv, 99, 119, 122, 127, 131, 133, 134, 135, 170*
On Crimes and Punishments 71, 158
open court *51, 64*
oppression *26, 40*
ordeal *35*
O'Sullivan, Patrick *169*
outlawry *110*

P

pain *76, 94*
Paine, Tom *89, 109, 165*
Paley, Archdeacon William *122, 123, 147*
Panopticon *160*
pardon *95, 109, 119, 121*
Parliament *21, 38, 39, 41, 47, 48, 64, 67, 68, 70, 84*
  Parliamentary supremacy *19*
passions *52, 72*
Patriot Act 2001 (USA) *xv, 152*
Peel, Robert *97, 130, 147*
penal law *126, 145*
perjury *135, 168, 169*
Peterloo Massacre *141*
Peters, Hugh *49*
Petition of Right *xiii, 41, 42, 44, 157*

Index

petty sessions *122*
pillory *128, 149*
pious perjury *119, 137*
Pitt, William *99, 110*
pity *52*
Platts Mills, John *170*
pleasure *94*
Polson, Archer *114*
precedent *20, 29, 41, 60, 70, 93*
prejudice *56*
prerogative *39, 43*
   prerogative courts *37, 51, 66*
   prerogative writ *69*
   royal prerogative *144, 157*
pressing to death *33, 51*
presumption of guilt *99*
presumption of innocence *24, 75, 96, 109, 123, 135*
Prevention of Terrorism Act 2005 *151*
Principles of Moral and Political Philosophy *122*
prison *80*
Prisoners' Counsel Act 1836 *137, 145, 165*
privacy *152*
Privy Council *33, 39, 69, 125*
procedure *67, 127*
Proclamations *39, 157*
Prohibition *37*
proof beyond reasonable doubt *99*
property *33, 51, 64, 66, 157*
protection of society *97*
protest *152, 167*
Prynne, William *40*
public meetings *113*
punishment *26, 61, 71, 72, 79, 80, 120, 121*
   certainty of *87*
   counter-crime *97*
   fear of punishment *75*
   harsh etc. punishments *71, 149*
   necessary punishments *87, 147*
   no punishment except by law *25*
   punishment is an evil *87*
   Rationale of Punishment *97*
Puritanism *47, 56*
Pym, John *40*

Q

Quarter Sessions *122, 168*
Queen Caroline *114*

R

rack *33*
radicalisation *125, 145*
Radzinowicz, Leon *95, 124, 132*
Raleigh, Walter *30*
rape *87*
Reading on Torture *144*
reason *74, 105*
   reasons of state *69, 70*
rebellion *26, 94*
reform *51, 58, 60, 73, 91, 92, 111, 112, 117, 142, 145, 148*
   breaking the sleep of centuries *147*
   Reform Act 1832 *141, 149*
   reformation of offenders *87, 121, 127*
   Reform Bill *125*

Remonstrance to the King 39
rendition 155
reparation
  to those found not guilty 127
repression 115
reprieves 121
restoration 51
  restoration of the monarchy 47
restraint 26
retaliation 87
Rich, Nathaniel 44
rights 67, 84, 157
  citizens' rights 64
  customary rights 93
  natural rights 85
  prisoners' rights 99, 132
  right of a people 113
  right to life 27
  right to silence 135
Rights of Man, The 109
rigidity 158
riot 57, 58, 59
Robertson, Geoffrey 133
Roget, Reverend John 119
Roman-canon law 32, 33, 111, 138, 157
Roman Catholic Church 75, 78, 118, 165
Romilly, Samuel xiv, 80, 92, 97, 113, 117, 123, 149, 162
Rosewall, Thomas 134
Rowles v. Mason 67
royal absolutism 32, 41
Royal Commission 142, 143
royal prerogative 29, 32, 36, 38
Ruins of Time, etc. 60

rule of law 19, 71, 87, 99, 107, 140, 151, 152, 157
  no closed category of cases xii
Rules of Conduct 158
rules of criminal evidence 97
Rump Parliament 50
Russell, Lord John 130, 145, 147, 148

S

Sandys, Duncan 172
Sawers, John 155
Scavenger's Daughter 33
Scotland 112
search 152
secrecy 76
  secret accusations 71, 75
  secret evidence 152
security 25, 88, 97, 123
  national 153
sedition 102, 107, 111, 170
  Seditious Meetings Bill 113
Selden, John 40, 69
self-incrimination 88, 135
severity 53, 120, 148
Shaftesbury, Lord 49
Sheridan, Richard Brinsley 113
Shoplifting Act 120
silence
  right to silence 24, 135
  silencing 105
slavery 97, 126
social contract 72

social, economic, cultural and political change *141*
social improvement *148*
sodomy *87*
Solicitor-General *40, 125*
solicitors *118, 167, 170*
sovereignty *67, 84*
  sovereign power *43*
special dispensations *87*
Special Jury *103, 106, 107, 109, 110*
Special Powers Act *99, 112*
spies *125, 155*
squires *141*
Stalin *66*
Star Chamber *37, 39, 51, 58, 108, 162*
state
  state trials *34, 99, 134*
Stephen, James Fitzjames *132*
Steyn, Lord *21, 25*
Stockdale, John *103*
Stuarts *32, 33, 64, 65, 144, 157*
suicide *153*
  suicide attacks *151*
Supreme Court *21, 68*
Supreme Court (USA) *153, 154*
surveillance *152*
"sus" *167*

T

Talbot, Francis Patrick *168*
taxation *45, 70*
terror *74, 99, 141*
  English Terror *99, 161*
terrorism *xv, xvi, 19, 20, 25, 151, 153*
  anti-terrorism legislation *22, 81*
  Prevention of Terrorism Act 2005 *25*
Thayer, James Bradley *132*
Thelwall, John *111, 112*
thief-takers *135, 137*
Thompson, E P *27*
Thoughts on Executive Justice *121*
torments *97*
torture *19, 27, 29, 33, 71, 74, 75, 80, 92, 95, 125, 138, 153, 155, 171*
  mental torture *95*
  tortures and torments *33*
  United Nations Convention Against Torture *154*
trade unions *141*
tradition
  bondage of noxious traditions *130*
transportation *97, 119, 127, 128, 147*
treason *34, 37, 86*
  constructive treason *57, 99*
  high treason *48, 57, 58, 77, 109, 134*
  interpretative treasons *58*
  Treason Act of 1352 *57, 58*
  treason trials *xiv, 30, 99, 110*
  Treason Trials Act 1696 *134*
Treaty on European Union *26*
trial
  prompt trial *159*
  speedy and public trial *88*
  speedy trial of juveniles *149*
  trial by peers *75*
tribunals *24*
truth *138*
Tudors *32, 33, 144*

Twining, Professor *96*
tyranny *26, 76, 98, 113, 118*

U

United States of America *20, 67, 68, 79, 152*
  Founding Fathers *41*
Universal Declaration of Human Rights *26*
Upper Court *48*
Utilitarianism *92, 96, 117, 149*
utility *93, 97*

V

violence *148*
Vogler, Richard *67*

W

Waltham Black Act *130*
waterboarding *81, 154*
Wentworth, Thomas *68*
White, Nicholas *119*
wicked and abominable laws *48*
Wilberforce, William *126*
wiretaps *152*
wisdom *124*
witchcraft *55, 56, 158*
witnesses *89*
Woolf, Lord *21*

Z

zeal *34*

www.ingramcontent.com/pod-product-compliance
Lightning Source LLC
Chambersburg PA
CBHW020329240426
43665CB00044B/1097